MW01107637

Stories from Christian Neighbors

A Heart for Ecumenism

Edited by
Vera Duncanson
Brian Johnson
Stefanie Weisgram, O.S.B.

LITURGICAL PRESS
Collegeville, Minnesota

www.litpress.org

1   2   3   4   5   6   7   8

Library of Congress Cataloging-in-Publication Data

Stories from Christian neighbors : a heart for ecumenism /
   edited by Vera Duncanson, Brian Johnson, Stefanie Weisgram.
         p.   cm.
   Includes bibliographical references.
   ISBN 0-8146-2349-2
   1. Ecumenical movement.   I. Duncanson, Vera.
II. Johnson, Brian.   III. Weisgram, Stefanie.

BX8.3.T45   2003
280'.042—dc21   2003044683

Contents

Acknowledgments

The stories of this book tell of hearts being shaped through the people, events, and places in our lives. While the conversations and writings of the participants became the heart of the book, the work of editing continued to shape, not only the book, but the hearts of the editors.

We met in a variety of settings, experiencing the gracious hospitality of our hosts. We are happy to acknowledge, with a great deal of gratitude, friends at:

Drake University, Des Moines, Iowa
Gustavus Adolphus College, St. Peter, Minnesota
The Chaplain's Office at Midway Airport, Chicago, Illinois
St. John's University, Collegeville, Minnesota
St. Benedict's Monastery, St. Joseph, Minnesota
St. Joseph's Abbey, Covington, Louisiana

Each place offered a new way of seeing as we sifted, ordered, and wove together the stories, writings, and conversations. We are grateful to our various readers and to the Lilly Foundation for providing the funds for us to move out from our own space, to encounter the experience and space of another—to do the work of ecumenism.

Vera Duncanson
Brian Johnson
Stefanie Weisgram, O.S.B.

Foreword

Let me begin the Foreword for this fine book by telling a little of my own ecumenical story. For over forty years I have been privileged to work in environments in which people from different Christian traditions found themselves together for various purposes. Sometimes I have gathered with others to work for some shared social cause. At other times I have been with people from different backgrounds studying in a theological school. Then there have been times of sharing the joys of weddings or the sorrows of funerals, occasions which so often gather people across faith traditions. The varied backgrounds of the staff working in my office have been another place of ecumenical connection. Finally, I have gathered many times with a diversity of people for the purpose of praying together amidst various social and personal crises, and also for the purpose of learning to pray more deeply.

An expansion of this last purpose: to pray together more deeply, has occupied most of my working life since 1973, when the Shalem Institute for Spiritual Formation was founded in Washington, D.C. (now Bethesda, Maryland). People from many different denominational commitments have come together in hundreds of Shalem contemplative formation and support groups since that time. We have come together to share the riches of contemplative tradition and practice that have threaded their way through all periods of Christian history. Contemplative tradition centers on a quality of immediate, loving presence to God in listening prayer and in prayerfully living through the happenings of our daily lives. We always have maintained respect for the denominational differences of those who come. At the same time we have seen a quality of shared spiritual hunger and an openness to various means of contemplative presence that have united those who come beyond their differences.

In Shalem's longer-term residential events, over meals and many casual conversations during the day outside of structured prayer and learning times, participants have discovered one another's humanness and faith stories in ways that have built long-term mutual trust and new perspectives on one another's denominational traditions. Many times I have felt that these ecumenical gatherings were called by God's Spirit, and were contributing to Christ's plea to God, "That they may all be one" (John 17:21). These groups have demonstrated that oneness amidst our diversity in numerous wondrous ways.

This book is full of such concrete stories of people's gripping ecumenical encounters with other people: amidst times of personal grief and need, in families, friendships, work relationships, and neighborhoods. These inspiring stories also include the personal ecumenical journey of some people, as their spiritual lives have been shaped through a number of different traditions. The stories emerge out of the meetings of a small group of Roman Catholics, Protestants, and Orthodox people, mostly lay, in Collegeville, Minnesota, over a three-year period. The group met out of a belief that we need to grow into virtues that enlarge our ecumenical heart, and this growth requires opportunities to meet Christians from Churches other than our own in order to pray together, and to share our faith stories, overlaps, and differences in a very personal and open way.

As these stories unfold related to a variety of chapter themes, readers are left at the end of each chapter with a number of personal questions to ponder about their own experience, understandings, and ways they can contribute to building bridges across faith traditions, while maintaining the integrity of their own. This makes the book particularly suitable as a shared stimulus for groups of people meeting across Christian faith lines. Such meetings require a personal centeredness on God and an openness to diversity as we listen to one another. The book lists many other particular ecumenical "virtues" that need to be nourished, for the sake of authentic relationships. At one point we are asked to look at those people who have mentored these virtues for us in our lives. We also are mentors for others, as they see us reaching out beyond our own faith tradition and showing an appreciation and respect for others.

Such open, prayer-filled encounters are not luxuries in our world today. In our fragile, interdependent island home, we desperately need to avoid the danger of embracing contempt for other historical Christian streams of tradition than our own, and an accompanying sense of our own faith's superiority and completeness. All members of the Body of Christ need to recognize how much we need the gifts that Christ's Spirit has showered on each part of the divided Body. In my long ecumenical experience, I often yearn for the strengths of our different traditions to be joined together, and the weaknesses to be shed. The formal realization of this realignment must await the Spirit's movements of the future, and even then, the realization will never be complete this side of heaven. But the encounters we have with one another across lines can contribute something to the greater fullness of all our traditions, as well as help us to live together with enough mutual appreciation and care that leads us to be blessings for one another and for the earth's peace.

This mutual respect and sharing, in turn, prepares us for a larger level of interfaith encounter: with Muslims, Jews, Buddhists, Hindus, Native Americans, and others. These, too, are our neighbors today, and we need to share through their stories the blessings and struggles they have known. We can trust that God's Spirit will be alive in such sharing, and draw us toward mutual enlargement of our spiritual traditions and toward a fuller sense of one human family, with many valuable and diverse ways of attending the holy.

Tilden Edwards
Shalem Institute
Bethesda, Maryland

Introduction

Ecumenical—The Word for the Twenty-First Century

Maggie said it well for all of us. "When I first agreed to attend this consultation, I was not sure what was expected of me. If I had to defend my stand, would I have to lose a bit of my identity through compromise? This would be, after all, ecumenical . . . doesn't one expect some loss in sacrifice to the cause of unity however slight?"

This is very likely how the word "ecumenical" strikes most people in the pews of our churches today. We aren't sure we "own" the word or the process. It belongs to those whom we perceive to "run" our churches. We surely have no part in it—nor do we want to. But the world is changing. The desire for peace is stronger than ever, both in our larger world and among peoples closer to home. This desire for peace might be personal for interior peace. It might be for peace in the world and nations around us. It might be for a kind of peace between denominations—even between the churches in our neighborhoods. Actions that bring about this kind of peace are what we can call "ecumenism," and it might frighten us when we realize it is our responsibility.

When she actually participated in the ecumenical consultation that had her wondering what she was getting into, Maggie was more than pleasantly surprised. She felt more whole and more enriched: "An agenda had shaped itself gently from the great amalgam of personal stories of weakness as well as of the strengths of each participant—friends actually—not simply participants. There were no confrontations but explorations. There were no defenses but revelations. . . . We had laughed uproariously with each other and we had wept together. . . . We didn't talk as much as listen. We enquired to understand, we suggested ways to explore personal gifts. We sang fugues and we sang in unison. We listened in silence and compassion. . . . We tasted the communion of love."

Ecumenism is not all sweetness and light, but entered into on the level of neighbors, it can bring rewards.

Where This Book Comes From

"I had a skinny ecumenical heart when I came here. It's getting bigger." What enlarged the skinny heart were conversations that took place for a week in each of three successive summers at the Institute for Ecumenical and Cultural Research, an independent center for study, reflection, and prayer in central Minnesota. Nineteen people—mostly lay persons, some clergy—were invited to discuss "Virtues for an Ecumenical Heart." These women and men came from all directions and from a variety of denominational backgrounds. All are involved in local churches. All were open, curious, and eager to talk and listen. This book is fashioned from the conversations.

The Institute is strongly influenced by its surroundings, Saint John's Abbey and Saint Benedict's Monastery. The Benedictines have practiced seeking God for fifteen hundred years, and have learned a thing or two in all that time. What they have most profoundly discovered, and offer to teach the rest of us, is this: Spontaneity requires discipline, to be free takes practice. The Rule of Saint Benedict puts it simply and powerfully: "As we progress in this way of life and in faith, we shall run on the path of God's commandments, our hearts overflowing with the inexpressible delight of love." A longing for "the inexpressible delight of love" is what serious Christians experience, often without words to express it.

The people who gathered at the Institute did not put it in this Benedictine way at the start. We were thinking we could make a list of principles that would characterize an ecumenical life. We would tell stories—stories from our lives—but the point would be to rise above the stories to a more general, abstract level. However, a more earthy wisdom prevailed. Real, daily life is where the virtues live; life is the virtues' natural habitat. Virtues are practices more than they are principles. You have to dig into the stories, not soar above them, to find the virtues.

Nobody could have predicted what happened. Plenary, small-group, and informal meetings took place, but nothing was programmed or controlled for a specific outcome. Talk was strictly first-person. Stories were of pain and joy, appreciation and regret, doubt and faith.

Stories are how we understand and explain our lives. They help us interpret what we see, hear, and feel. Stories teach us life lessons, how to interpret the present in terms of the past, and hint at ways to prepare for the future. They enable us to express gratitude in a creative way.

The stories told grew in importance and were revisited over and over during the three summers, often with new understandings and appreciation. Honoring difficult stores became imperative. During the third summer the stories resulted in a variety of writings: anecdotes, meditations, poems, essays, character sketches. This book is formed around these writings. Different voices, different stories, one vision's hope for ecumenical conversation in all sorts of places, and an eagerness to visit—maybe even inhabit—the surprising new places where those conversations might lead.

This book is addressed to all persons, laity and clergy alike, who want to live and share their faith, to anyone who is interested, open, and willing to reach out. One consultation participant put it this way: "Ecumenism is the opposite of living within narrow walls of your own house. It's reaching across." Reaching across deepens friendships even while it builds common understandings. We can put more effort into what binds us together than into what separates us. Reaching across diminishes our fears and increases our appreciation of our own gifts when we see them through the eyes of others. In sum, reaching across makes us more complete, because when we are together we are more than the sum of our parts.

What You Will Find in This Book

The stories, memories, and reflections of the participants in the consultation are the substance of this book. As we pondered the materials, one story would remind us of another, and soon the stories grouped themselves.

Part I. Beginning

Chapter 1. Gathering Neighbors

Here we introduce the idea of ecumenical neighbors, whom we see—and who see us—with new eyes.

Chapter 2. Exchanging Stories

Stories reveal our innermost self, where we come from, what from the past or present motivates us today. We discover commonalities even while we appreciate differences.

Chapter 9. Envisioning Hope

Hope breaks through over and over again in each chapter. Here we see how hope wins out—with imagination and humor.

What We Hope This Book Will Do

If Christians are to grow into virtues that enlarge our ecumenical hearts, we can't do it alone or in the privacy of our own church. Timothy Kelly, O.S.B., former abbot of Saint John's Abbey, states the challenge and opportunity. "If the Body of Christ on earth is to be a community of believers, then communication is essential to communion. The relationship of a person to God may well be very personal, but it can never be private. Who we are with God cannot be separated from who we are with one another, and it is as the body of humanity that we have the potential for becoming the Body of Christ."

We need opportunities to meet Christians from churches other than our own. We need to sit down with them and know them—really know them, not them as we imagine them to be. We need courage to share our beliefs and discover both what we have in common and how we differ. We need to let go of any fear we have that they might be right and we might be wrong. We need to share our personal faith stories, our search for God, our experience of love in community, and even our faith problems and sorrows. We need to pray together and let the Spirit work within and among us. This is what happened in Collegeville.

We hope that you will find this book useful and helpful, but we have to give this warning: Ecumenism is not a program, not a quick fix. Stories don't tell you what to do. If they work, they trigger your own telling of your own story in light of the challenge and blessing. No one can do the work of Christian unity for you, but we can assure

you that it is work that you can do. It is enormously grati-
fying—and sometimes even hard—and worth it. When
people finally got the point of Jesus' stories, he told them
to go and do likewise. We want to borrow his words and
say the same to you. We believe the Gospel will be served
if other Christians read what we say and start talking
with each other in the same way.

Part I
Beginning

Chapter 1

Gathering Neighbors

"For where two or three are gathered in my name,
I am there among them."
Matthew 18:20

"Bring yourself, bring your life." The Institute didn't ask us to prepare papers or speeches. In fact, it asked us *not* to. Most of us were strangers to one another. We arrived with a common longing and a suitcase full of stories. We had a common heritage—the story of our faith.

It did not take long to become neighbors. Everybody has an idea of what makes neighbors—meeting in the yard while planting tomatoes, taking a casserole after a death, buying Girl Scout cookies, having coffee, turning on the porch light for Halloween, tolerating differences, celebrating parts of the journey—in short, moving out from our own space and history. Someone has to extend a hand. The Institute, in its beautiful Minnesota setting complete with loons on the lake, gathered us out of our own families and history.

Mr. Rogers' Neighborhood, on public television, gathers children and teaches them about being a good neighbor by introducing them to all sorts of individuals who together provide a safe and caring community where people of all ages can create, love, and grow. He invites his audience to see the ways we are connected, how we depend on one another. *Mr. Rogers' Neighborhood* nurtures young, ecumenical hearts. Imagine the gentle voice of Fred Rogers—who is, by the way, a Presbyterian minister—coaxing, "Please, won't you be my neighbor?" as he exchanges his dress shoes and jacket for an old worn sweater and sneakers.

Wherever we might have come from, we are now in a place of curiosity, imagination, sharing, and friendship. "Where two or three are gathered in my name, I am there among them," we have been promised.

So, we extend a hand and offer a cup of coffee. We invite you to bring your own story as you listen to ours. First, though, we want to tell you what we did. Here is how Brian sums it up.

> We gathered around a question.
>
> Our lives lived in the promise of God were the answers.
>
> One by one, we began to tell the stories that have shaped our becoming—building trust, developing intimacy, and sharing the range of human emotions.
>
> The uncommon commonality was not the confession of a particular belief, nor the need to know a confessional position, but rather, we confessed truth about our lives, not expecting absolution from each other, but rather, finding resolution in the common need we all have to question and discover.
>
> Coming from somewhere means something—generic belief is not the goal. Celebrating, commiserating, and rehearsing the moments that even though are subtle and elusive, suggest that the Spirit is at work.
>
> We have been witnesses.

What will come of this time together? We will never know and perhaps always know. Developing an ecumenical heart is like the water that begins a waterfall—a drop at a time. Virtue after virtue, mentor after mentor, experience after experience contribute to the momentum.

We are at the heart of the matter. The paradox of being and becoming compels each of us to keep searching with each other as companions.

"Coming from somewhere means something." We journey from diverse neighborhoods.

Many of us grew up in homes with several religious identities—a Presbyterian father, a Methodist mother; Catholic parents, Lutheran cousins; Southern Baptist mother, "cynical atheist father"; mother Evangelical Free Church, father Methodist, joined in the Church of the Nazarene, and so forth.

Others were born into closely bound enclaves—Swedish Lutheran, Greek Orthodox, Roman Catholic.

Some of us left our faith traditions and returned; others have tried several denominations in search of home. Several had parents and grandparents who were ministers. One was "disfellowshiped and disinvited" from her lifelong tradition.

Our neighborhoods include AA tables, dying patients, theology classes, business transactions, libraries, struggling children, works of art, grandparenting. Our neighborhoods have much in common, but are rooted in rich histories of their own.

"The different denominations are guarding certain charisms," said one. "What I bring is more than myself; I bring the shoulders I stand on." Christian neighbors bring unique gifts to any ecumenical gathering: history, traditions, ways of knowing God, styles of worship, familiar hymns, wisdom gleaned from teachers, companions, books, prayer. Ecumenism is not about abandoning individual traditions or erasing the carefully crafted beauty and character of a neighborhood in order to create a new one. "Generic belief is not the goal," but rather "recognizing God in the other tradition."

"Autonomy and self-sufficiency are not ecumenical virtues. My tradition makes no sense in and of itself, apart from relationship to other Christian churches," says Gary. "Incompleteness drives me into desire for relationship with other persons and traditions." Neighborhood gatherings can lead to a realization of our need for one another's gifts. We exchanged these gifts in our conversations, morning and evening prayer, late night talks, walks around the lake, eating together.

What calls diverse Christians together? The Word of God? The Spirit of God? The Love of God? "We gathered around a question," but sometimes it is the search for God which gathers us.

"I didn't start looking for God's people," Tim said. "I wanted to get closer to God. My object was not to acquire an ecumenical heart; the heart was a surprise."

Coming to know God must sooner or later lead us to one another. Love of God and love of neighbor are inseparable, yet we have lived much of our Christian history isolated from one another. But Carol was always quick to point out that in spite of the tales of separation, rich stories of unity also exist in our communities as we gather to share food, choirs, money for those in need, celebration, grief. Those stories, especially, need to be acknowledged and celebrated.

> In small towns we tend to think of community as just the place where we live, nothing special about it. I live in Foley, Minnesota. Much of the time we down-

play who we are and how we live our lives. But a new mural on the exterior of a local business and emblazoned on t-shirts proclaims that "Foley is a good place." I agree.

Foley is a place where we care about one another. We care about our older folk and we care very much for our children. We are people of faith. I suspect that very few people would think of themselves as ecumenists. In Foley we "just do it."

The CROSS Center (Christians Reaching out in Social Service) is a food shelf and clothing distribution center supported by all denominations. The volunteers come as individuals. They came with hammers to help build a Presbyterian church. A seventy-voice ecumenical choir presents a Palm Sunday concert annually. One year the concert proceeds supported the new Presbyterian building. The same choir came to sing and stayed to celebrate as that new building was dedicated. Another year the concert benefited a Roman Catholic child needing a heart transplant, and the following year it honored the memory of a teacher killed in an accident.

All the children of the community are invited to attend Vacation Bible Schools in the Protestant churches. The Presbyterian youth programs serve all who want to come. The annual Roman Catholic bazaar and the Lutheran fall supper are major community events. Smaller fundraising events, ice cream socials, and soup suppers are widely supported.

We come together in worship at weddings, often marrying across denominational lines, and we come together in worship to bury friends and family. The ministers of the area served as honorary pallbearers at the funeral Mass of the local funeral director.

> Is this ecumenism? It most certainly is. It is the best kind of ecumenism—natural, not forced, but flowing from a shared love of Christ and respect for one another and the Church universal.

Christian neighbors in Foley, Minnesota, have cared enough to carve out of their busy lives time, space, and occasions for gathering. That is a huge commitment for people who sometimes barely have enough time to attend their own church on Sunday mornings. Creating time to gather is a challenge, but an even greater challenge is slowing down enough to see one another as whole human beings and integral parts of the Body of Christ.

"Our tendency is to be premature about what we see," Alva said. "We need to slow ourselves down, suspend judgment, allow things to become clearer. We can continue to move, with commas rather than periods." Loving, honest neighbors sometimes point this out to us, as Pedro was able to in a story Stefanie told us.

> I am an inveterate people-watcher. When I go to Guatemala for my yearly stint of volunteer library work—and the recharging of my spiritual battery—I especially like to watch the pilgrims who come to the basilica to venerate at the shrine of the Black Christ. I like to watch the faces and see their faith, to listen to the prayers and hear their faith. I have come to love the people of Guatemala more by watching them than by anything else.

> Several years ago a Guatemalan friend was here in Minnesota studying. While he was here, our diocesan paper came out with what turned out to be a Catholic Press award-winning photo article about a village in Guatemala. When I saw the large-spread article, I was immediately excited and thought that Pedro would be delighted to see it.

When I showed it to him, his reaction took me by surprise. As he looked over the article and the photos carefully, I could see something building up in him. I asked him what he thought, and he exploded.

"Look at this! See what you do to us! You use our poverty against us! You take photos showing how poor we are and how poorly we live, and you say this is Guatemala and the Guatemalan people. But you aren't seeing the whole truth. Yes, we are poor, but we are more! We have joy and happiness. We love and we are loved—just like you! Don't look at our poverty. Look at our faces if you want to see us. Then you will see our joy and our generosity and our happiness. We are more than a poor people; we are a happy people! We aren't different from you. We are like you; happy and sad, loving and joyful!"

That was a meditation for me. Of course he was right. They are like us—whole people with all the emotions, gifts, problems, and graces we all have. I am often reminded of this when I meet new people who are different from me, whether in gender, race, sexual orientation, religious tradition. It changes how I react and how I think and how I accept.

My vision was shortsighted before this sobering interaction with Pedro. Now more than ever I try to look at faces and remember that we all have so much more in common as human beings, all children of the same God, regardless of what name we use for that God.

In the past, Christians have struggled with issues of doctrine, theology, Scripture interpretation, worship—often focusing on things that divide. Many of us, however, are not even aware of the issues being debated. For nearly

2,000 years we have tried to understand and live out the message of Jesus and his followers, but what does it mean to be one and live together as children of the same God? Gathering neighbors after centuries of isolation is not easy.

We arrived with our own anxieties and fears, as Maggie wrote: "I was not sure what was expected of me. If I had to defend my stand, would I have to lose a bit of my identity through compromise?" Fears subsided as we became friends. We did not experience a compromise of our individual identities, but rather a celebration and appreciation of them. "Doors have glided open quietly," Maggie continued, "windows have lifted up silently, and the bells of the monastery affirm our oneness. And at night when I am reading or just about to fall asleep, the plaintive cry of nature's oboes—the loons—ask why it is not always this way."

Further thinking:

1. On what occasions do you gather with your family? Church? Neighborhood?

2. Nurture a conversation with another person about his or her neighborhood.

3. What gifts do you bring to ecumenical occasions?

4. Ask your pastor or a member of your congregation what ecumenical gatherings are occurring.

Chapter 2

Exchanging Stories

"I will open my mouth to speak in parables; I will proclaim
what has been hidden from the foundation of the world."
Matthew 13:35b

Many of us find ourselves in a video store on Friday
evening—we're too tired from a week's work to go out
but are desperately in search of a good story. We look to
movies, magazines, television, books, hoping for a story
that captures our imagination. Some of us are "people-
watchers." We enjoy observing others at airports, malls,
or wherever people just being themselves meander—parents loaded down with bags and children, exotic looking
couples, loners. We begin to imagine their stories, their
histories.

We look for stories in distant places, but are often un-
aware of the rich stories of those close by—coworkers,
family members, the person sitting next to us at church,
the congregation down the street. Americans confess to
not knowing the neighbor next door. For years this has
been the case among Christian churches, though we've
seldom confessed it. We have observed one another from

a distance, heard one another's music from across the street, but have not followed our curiosity through the church doors. It is time to show ourselves to one another—and we do this best through storytelling.

We love a story—our common heritage lies in stories—yet we create few opportunities for storytelling. Gather together a family, a group of children, a youth group, a clergy group, any group, drop a question or suggestion into the mix, and the stories that emerge are like ripples in a pond. This is how we came to see and be seen, but any group can do it. "Tell us about your life as a process of discovering and cultivating the virtues of an ecumenical heart in yourself and others," we were asked the evening we arrived.

The next morning one of us asked God to bless our stories, and over the next two days we told them, in the first person, one by one—strangers exchanging stories, being changed in the process. The stories themselves were being changed through the giving and receiving, the telling and the listening, the pauses and silences.

For Carol, breakthrough came when God moved out of the box.

> In 1984 I began my journey toward recovery from alcoholism. I began that journey with thirty-two days at Hazelden in Center City, Minnesota. When first introduced to the Twelve Steps, I felt quite confident, even superior to my peers. After all, I had a strong belief in God. Soon it became apparent that my understanding of God was inadequate for the business of recovery.
>
> God is a "given" in the Twelve Steps. The challenge was to come to an understanding of just who God is for me and how God works in my life. The treatment process left time for the personal reflection and study

that I needed, and it was clear that I had permission to start the struggle.

In retrospect, I see that my complete powerlessness (Step One) drove me to seek God in a more personal way than I had previously known was possible. I felt vulnerable and free at the same time. For the first time in my life it was apparent that God is understood by people in many different ways and that's okay. God started to move out of the box.

My recovery continued with the help of many others who sit around Twelve Step tables. We gather for one common purpose: to recover from alcoholism. No one is an authority, and all discussion is in the first person. We come with our own experience, strength, and hope, to talk about what it was like, what happened, and what it is like now. I bring the God of my understanding to the table, and I must allow others to bring the God of their understanding.

Viewing God from the perspective of another, gathering the understandings of God around the table, requires that we see, as Mary Jane says, with "an artist's eye."

I felt an artistic, creative energy emanating from all the people in our group. I remember Susan saying, "When we share stories, we share our vision with one another." That is what we did, and that is what artists do, whatever their medium.

The artist looks for patterns, forms, and tries to find cohesiveness amidst chaos. The artist sits loose to ideology so can usually connect with universals and images that are recognized by human beings everywhere. The artist has other virtues of the ecumenical heart—those of seeing and listening. The artist must be observant and listen well in order to reflect her vision and world.

The poet especially tries to capture an experience that precedes language and hence avoids that barrier, looking for something that is almost pre-verbal, therefore more universal. In the process of being creative, a person is freed from normal restrictions and is able to see more clearly and thoroughly.

The poet, storyteller, painter, sculptor, musician, playwright, actor, dancer—they all communicate with talents that are not readily available to many of us. But we all can develop the virtues of the artist. We can develop the artist's eye and open ourselves to revelation and the wider truths. These are surely virtues of an ecumenical heart.

Curt is a businessman with an artist's eye. He embraces curiosity, skepticism, and flexibility—"Something is there you don't see, and something you see isn't there"—that invite the stories of others and lead one outward.

Much of my love for ecumenism comes from my personality trait of curiosity and of trying to find a better way. Since the time I was a small child, I have had a strong curiosity about how things work, why they work that way or were designed a certain way, and if there is a better way. I love to learn and do research on topics of interest to me.

In the church I grew up in, I didn't feel there was a flexibility of faith. There seemed to be an unwillingness to address ideas from other faiths, with no explanation for the diversity of religions.

I think my adverse reaction to the fundamentalist faith structure caused me to inquire into other faiths, and at the same time to be aware of shortcomings as well as strengths. I find it very hard to really bite on a particular faith.

At the end of *Annie Hall* Woody Allen tells the story of a man who says to his psychiatrist, "My brother thinks he is a chicken." The psychiatrist says, "Why don't you tell your brother he's not a chicken?" The patient responds, "I don't want to tell him he's not a chicken because we need the eggs."

I've often felt that churches preach a theology that just doesn't produce the eggs. "If you just live this way, or believe that way, your life will be this way." "If you accept Christ as your personal Savior, you will have life everlasting." Perhaps because I don't understand life after death, I question its reality. This is what I mean by "seeing something that isn't there."

At the same time, I think I sometimes lose sight of the presence of God in our daily lives, of where God shows up in our relationships and in our community. This is the "something is there that you don't see."

I had a dream the other night about morphing, changing shapes into many forms. It seems to be a reflection of the process of learning about faith and God, forming opinions and taking positions, then finding those positions inadequate. A morphing occurs in my life as I explore a new approach and start the process over.

Living stories lined up side by side take on a common rhythm and pattern: Who am I? Who are my people? How did we get from here to there? Stories of exclusion, inclusion, revelation—we exchanged all of them, and little by little we began to see our own story in the story of the other.

Herb: I was born into a Swedish Lutheran enclave. We had nothing to do with Norwegian or German Lutherans. I didn't know any theological difference;

only about beer. Germans drank, Norwegians didn't, and Swedes did but behind closed shades. . . . I should have gone to college at Gustavus Adolphus (Swedish Lutheran), but went to Augsburg, run by Norwegians. Some of the professors helped me see that if you're going to be a Christian, you've got to live in the world.

Alva: In my church in Dallas we celebrate in a lively way. Our sacred dance concerts and choir trips involve members from different traditions. African American churches have been ecumenical by nature. My pastor said to his brother, who gave as an excuse for not going to church in the Bay Area that there wasn't a convenient Methodist church, "Go to any church if there's not a Methodist church around." I value this kind of boldness in the faith.

Maggie: Both my parents came over from Greece. I was born in Iowa in a little Greek enclave. We were all "going to go back" after we'd made enough money. Nobody went back, and we were stuck with all this preparation. Just stepping out of the enclave was an ecumenical experience. Besides learning about other Americans, I went to a Catholic college. In an enclave you don't pick up prejudices because you're totally removed. The Catholic environment was accepting.

Susan: My first ecumenical experience was in grade school in Kansas City. I grew up Catholic and went to parochial school. I had Lutheran relatives in Minnesota and spent summers there. I went to my cousin's confirmation, remembering what I'd been taught: "You don't participate in other people's church services." Do I stand or sit? I was amazed to find out they had to memorize the same questions and answers about the creed as we did. I was being taught separateness, but experiencing much more commonality.

Moments of revelation may enter a journey at any point through any medium. The longings of a young girl are as valuable as the thoughts of a competent minister, and serve as rich ground for revelation. A letter of encouragement or the whisper of God may find its way to us as it did to Nancy, if we are open to being found.

I always wanted to do something big for God. This longing began early in my life. In seventh grade I kept the disciplines of the faith by reading my Bible and praying daily. I remember struggling with the big questions: Who was I? What was my place in the world?

News of the race riots was finding its way into my life. I could not understand why my church was not talking about this horror. Every night I took newspaper and magazine articles and spread them across my bed. In my nightly prayers I prayed for peace and I prayed for guidance for what I might do.

One day I decided to write to President Kennedy. I poured out my heart to him in a twelve-page letter. I remember telling him that if he needed my help to get the word out about equality and love for all, I was available.

The day came for a special visit to my hometown of the President and the First Lady. Midday during school, we received the news that President Kennedy had been shot and killed just a few miles away. We were all sent home. When I walked in the door of my home, there was my whole family huddled around the television. Along with millions around the world, we were trying to take in this terrible tragedy.

I found my place on the floor. My mother got up and reached for a letter on the TV. She handed it to me and said, "Nancy, you got a letter today." I took it and read the top left hand corner. It was from the White House. My long-awaited reply had finally come to me.

The letter encouraged me to do all I could to work for peace and an end to prejudice and hatred. It was a defining moment. It was a moment of revelation. There was no turning back. I knew then the big thing that I could do for God.

Sometimes "being found" involves "being found"—a common theme in our stories. Dan exemplifies competence, faithfulness, and a lifetime of serving God and the people of God in leadership positions, yet he teaches all of us about humility and our need for those who are different from us. Allowing our true selves, flawed selves, whole selves to be seen is a risky business, and yet ecumenical hearts thrive on this kind of vulnerability and openness.

When I was eight, I stuck out my foot at a birthday party and tripped the birthday-girl as she ran by with a plate full of cake and ice cream. As she lay sprawling and bawling, I saw that everyone had seen me do it. Two feelings still linger—my utter shame and my utter inability to account for what I'd done.

I grew up believing I was more real when in control of events around me and feelings inside. Surprises were to be avoided. When they happened, they were my fault. Free expression of feelings, even pleasant ones, was unseemly—even dangerous! In a culture where surprises and feelings were exceptions, shame and confusion were frequent companions.

Many influences since have countered that original life command to increase control and mute feelings, but none more forcefully than my daughter Cynthia.

I used to call Cynthia "our humanizing influence." She was born with a heart defect which, although repaired, took her life thirty-six years later. Whatever caused her physical problem also left her with a mild learning disability, which one author calls the "hidden handicap." It was accompanied by emotional issues which in turn sparked concerns in parenting and led to counseling.

When I called the counselor to set up an initial appointment, he asked, "What's going on?" I described our parenting concerns with Cynthia and said, "I want to understand her better so I can be a more effective parent." He replied simply, "She's not the issue, you are."

I was incensed. How could he know? How dare he, on a first phone call! I almost ended it there, but agreed to come in. It turned out he was right, which, I realized later, is why I called Cynthia our humanizing influence. My counseling went on for eight years and was fundamental to my emerging new self-understanding.

With all her problems, or what we call problems, and the suffering which went with them, Cynthia was a gifted natural musician, a fun-loving party nut, an empathetic caretaker, and an explosive expresser of feelings. Her death left a huge hole in my heart. Many times a day I am reminded of her by laughter or crying, by bright colors or a parade, by something I know she'd like, or by someone I know she would relate to.

If there's a scale of being more-or-less-human, Cynthia redefined it for me.

The elderly, those who are ill and those who are dying in our communities, sometimes tell their stories with a sense of urgency. As they seek to make sense of their lives and put things in order, they also long to be remembered, hope they have made a difference, and wish to express gratitude. Stefanie relates how exchanging stories may increase gratitude in the teller and the listener, for our own story and that of the other.

> I had a friend who had lived for many years with a rare form of cancer. On several occasions when he came to the United States from his monastery in Central America, he came to my monastery first before visiting his family. Supposedly he was coming for a short retreat, but in truth he came to talk about what was happening in his Central American country, the atrocities, the killings, the torture, and the dangers he had been involved in, by force of conscience, in helping those being persecuted. He had to get it all out of his system before he could be at peace while with his family.
>
> When it became obvious that his cancer could no longer be controlled, his stories changed. Now he spoke of his life, from childhood to young adulthood to middle age. The stories poured from him: happy, sad, joyous, regretful, humorous, outraged, grateful. If I interrupted except for clarification, he would say with urgency, "Let me speak!" The storytelling intensified when I spent three months in Guatemala. A few weeks before I left, my friend ended a story and said, "Now I am finished. That is the last story."
>
> When I returned to Minnesota, I spoke with a community member about this experience of storytelling. She told me that she had the same experience with her mother as well as with many of our older com-

munity members. She had given this some thought and had come to the realization that the storytelling was very likely a way of expressing gratitude for a person's life.

In telling the stories, my friend could look back in appreciation, savoring his lifetime. In sharing what had made up the years of his life, he was showing me but also showing God that he treasured his life and was grateful for all he had experienced. He had to bear witness to his life and to his gratitude. I had to be a witness—a privileged witness.

With all their pain and joy, our stories spill out. Often when we think we are giving straight information we are revealing and expressing gratitude. Stories celebrate what we have and what we have been given. When we share stories of our faith traditions, we hear of pain and sorrow, of faithfulness and joy. Again we are moved to gratitude—for what I have, for what you have, for what we have together. This gratitude enables us to take risks as well as to engage in hard work together, to move forward in hope and trust out of the richness we have received.

To move forward in hope requires patience. We do not all experience the same sense of urgency as those who have a life-threatening disease. If religious institutions ever witnessed the tunnel and light of near-death experiences, perhaps they would be inclined to move with just a little more urgency; but both the impatient and patient stories need to be valued and exchanged. To her surprise, others recognized in Carol the virtue of patience, and asked her to write about it.

I think of myself as an impatient person. In fact I consider impatience to be one of my primary character defects. The suggestion that I might have the virtue of patience is quite a shock to my system. Is this another fruit of the recovery process?

If I have it, that is where I found it. Step Three, "Made a decision to turn our will and lives over to the care of God *as we understood Him,*" has changed the way I operate. When faced with a situation that I cannot and should not control, I am far more able to "turn it over" than I was able to do in my pre-recovery life. It has been a tremendous relief to give up the burden of making God's decisions.

The *Serenity Prayer* seemed an overly simplistic solution to life's problems when I first began recovery. The older—and I hope wiser—me has sense enough to use it frequently as a guide to understanding just what belongs on my plate and what belongs on God's. "God, grant me the serenity to accept the things I cannot change, to change the things I can, and the wisdom to know the difference."

Step Eleven, "Sought through prayer and meditation to improve our conscious contact with God *as we understood Him,* praying only for knowledge of His will for us and the power to carry that out," has given me—a good, orderly Presbyterian—a procedure to follow as I strive to continue this growth spurt in understanding God, myself, and life.

How does this all relate to ecumenism? These three principles, Step Three, the *Serenity Prayer,* and Step Eleven, apply directly to the way I work for Christian unity. I try to be aware of just what can't be changed right now. I try to identify just what I can change and where I might influence change. Most important, I attempt to remember that God is in charge. My job is to ask God to reveal the path I must walk and to give me the power to walk it. When I am able to do all of this, I am filled with hope. If this is patience, so be it.

Ecumenism happens as we exchange stories that allow us to look for commonalities, appreciate differences, witness pain, share hope, express anger, reconcile, be surprised, kindle imagination, see God in a new way, laugh, love, heal. Clergy exchange pulpits. High school students exchange countries. When Christians exchange stories, individuals are changed, understanding is deepened, and surely God must be pleased.

The stories of ordinary lives are worthy of telling and exchanging. Somewhere along the way we have allowed Hollywood to become our storyteller, defining for us a "good story," a "worthy teller." Cracking open stories is essential for ecumenism to happen, on any level.

Further thinking:

1. Who taught you about tolerance or encouraged you to imagine?

2. Tell a story from your life about curiosity, inclusion, exclusion, loss, imagination.

3. Tell about an experience when you received or sent a letter of encouragement or received a whisper from God.

4. When have you been in a position of receiving or giving up control?

Chapter 3
Confronting Challenges

"Fight the good fight of the faith; take hold of the eternal life,
to which you were called and for which you made the good
confession in the presence of many witnesses."
1 Timothy 6:12

It isn't easy for Christians to talk about the hard things. For some people, conflict is anti-Christian. Disagreement is ignored and avoided. Differences of opinion are taboo. Ecumenical hearts recognize the inherent risks in conflict, yet they also know that it is inevitable to be opposed to each other. In ecumenical dialogue, someone has to lead the way, to take the risk of addressing what is difficult. As we sat around the table for the first conversation, however, it didn't take long to start naming experiences that were painful, frustrating, or challenging. For many of us, an ecumenical heart grew through challenge.

Brian lost his home in a tornado which radically altered the landscape of the college community of which he is a part.

> After the winds that destroyed many homes and damaged many buildings, the college community was sur-

prised, I think, by the impact of this event on how people relate to one another. During the days immediately following the storm, individuals on opposite sides of issues in departments or divisions, who used to be unable to talk with or face each other, were now speaking. Long-held grudges began to evaporate. Students angry with a roommate were now ready to talk.

As a college community, we utilize many texts on campus. But we had not been able to share a common text of experience for many years. Communities sometimes share a common history or join to create a common vision of the future, yet seldom are they afforded the opportunity to be authentic in their common needs and honest about their fears and vulnerabilities. This common text makes it possible to communicate with each other through the power of our individual stories. Ecumenical hearts know that to welcome these stories is how we celebrate our common text of belief in Jesus Christ.

Stories of death and loss create opportunities for ecumenical heart work. Herb remembered how his family had taught him to be suspicious of a particular faith tradition, and how the suspicion dissipated at the funeral of his son. As the procession was leaving the church, someone stepped out into the aisle to greet him with an embrace of care. It was someone of the tradition he was supposed to be wary of. We can meet each other in our grief in ways that are impossible in other settings.

Curt, an entrepreneur and committed ecumenist, found that within every denomination there are those who find room to cultivate the virtues of an ecumenical heart. The risk of this challenge, while not hurtful or frustrating, engendered anxiety for Curt and created an opportunity for his heart to be opened to possibility and the Spirit.

"I'd like to recommend your name for nomination as a deacon." An associate pastor of our church was calling to see if I was interested.

I always was able to sidestep differences in theology that I felt between my own beliefs and the "party line" of the denomination. I knew I had some disagreements with the confessions of our church, but I was sure I needed to be in some church and this one was more appealing than others I had visited. The denomination was similar to the tradition in which I was raised. Many of my best friends attended the church. The programs and preaching were excellent. I thought these were all good reasons to join this particular church.

When it regularly came time to read the confessions in church, I always knew I didn't believe them completely. But it was not enough of a conflict to keep me from saying the words. The phone call brought the conflict to the front burner. "What kind of church would this be if the officers didn't believe what they were confessing? Would I want to be a member of a church that had leaders with the lack of integrity I was showing? Could I say those confessions again and still feel like I had any integrity at all?"

All these questions swirled around in my mind as I pondered the request. When I couldn't figure it out, I called the pastor-in-residence, temporarily serving our church as we sought a new senior pastor. He set an appointment, and soon I was in his office discussing my problem.

We pulled books down from the shelves and read the confessions required of a deacon, considering word by word the statements and their meaning. I could see that I was interpreting the words in a more strict and literal way than he was. I began to feel that perhaps I could agree with the statements. But the final convincing came when he told me, "If you have questions about these theological issues, then you are our kind of guy. It's the people who have it all figured out that worry me."

I did accept that nomination and became a deacon. I found that I could have questions about my church's theology and still keep my integrity. With the mentoring of this pastor, I was able to validate my own faith and at the same time serve the church. I found there was enough "wiggle room" in the church for me, and it allowed people of differing opinions to join together to serve God.

Even to be able to *admit* the need for growth brings new insight. A challenging situation not only nurtures necessary growth but also brings new insight and reflectiveness about our common humanity. Dan, a pastor and former national Church leader, wrote about the transformation that is encouraged by conflict.

It was a powerful and painful learning experience. I was one of eighteen church executives, male and female, in a weeklong workshop on gender dynamics in the workplace. The title of the workshop was "Women and Men Working Together in the Church." The lectures integrated understandings I already had and dispelled puzzling mysteries I'd always wondered about. The exercises were revealing and provocative.

A simulation game climaxed the week. The object was to dispose of thirty-six dollars collected from the participants. It couldn't go to charity but had to benefit the group or a member of it.

We were divided into two groups, an inner circle and an outer circle. The inner circle would do the negotiating. Each member of the inner circle was paired with a "consultant" in the outer circle, mixing men and women. There would be three time-limited negotiation rounds, and between them, those from the inner circle would huddle with their consultants. In the end, the clock forced a decision.

I ended up consultant to an inner-circle woman—my chance to demonstrate my enlightened understanding of men-women dynamics. Each round was noisier than the last as the excitement escalated. I forget what was done about the money, but I'll never forget how the postmortem revealed that, at every step, I had instructed my client on what to do next. I thought I had acted in an enlightened way but was caught in the act of assuming that without me she had no chance. I was totally and tearfully unmasked by my own behavior.

It was one of the most profound learning moments of my life. For one thing, I learned to trust the community more and my own assumptions less.

Another interaction left Patrick stunned by the prescribed way in which systems and institutions train us in mistrust of each other.

It was a month after H. C. (Bob) Piper's funeral. He had died of cancer at age seventy-one. As chair of my board, he had been my boss for six years. He was one of Minnesota's movers and shakers, known for his business savvy and his generosity. He built the family firm into a flagship of the investment trade, and contributed annually to more than one hundred thirty institutions and charities. He gave personally, and he persuaded his firm to set the standard for

Minnesota's nationally recognized level of corporate philanthropy.

At age fifty, he had earned a master's degree from United Theological Seminary of the Twin Cities while continuing to run the company. Bob would sometimes say, "I know how to make things happen." Working closely with somebody who had his sort of initiative kept me alert.

We were four at table, reminiscing about this man whose life had affected us in countless ways. One, a foundation executive, told of an occasion, many years before, when Bob had come to him seeking a grant for a nonprofit that Bob was raising money for. "I wish I could help, but the foundation's guidelines rule out grants to such institutions." "Well, show me a list of your board members." Bob looked at the list, recognized several names, and said, "I'm going to go straight to them." He did, but the board members stood behind their executive. Bob let the executive know that he was furious. The executive then finished the reminiscence: "A few weeks later Bob and I were at a social event, and he came up to me and was the soul of cordiality."

My instinctive reaction was to think, "Yes, that's the business world; smiling, smiling, while still being a villain." But my reaction was not in the deepest sense instinctive. It was a trained academic prejudice. And I'm very glad I didn't say it, because I would have sounded the fool I was.

Another of my table companions said, "Yes, that's because Bob Piper knew what every good business person knows. You never burn your bridges behind you, because you never know when you might have to cross them again."

Suddenly I knew: One of the pathologies of the academic life (and it goes for life in churches, too) is the endless bearing of grudges. In the years since leaving the professorial ranks, I have had numerous dealings with business people, encounters that I have found on the whole to be refreshing, but I hadn't understood why. Now I know that it's partly because people in that line of work live by what I have long thought a recipe for sanity and health, some words that Erasmus attributes to Folly: "They make mistakes together or individually (and) wisely overlook things."

We think progress depends on getting it right and being accountable. There is much to be said for correctness and responsibility. The story about Bob Piper at the party taught me that there is also much to be said for making mistakes and wisely overlooking things, among our churches as well as in the business world.

Conflicts exist with and between Christian traditions. But the need for ecumenical and open hearts can be most challenging within a tradition where it is often most needed. Nancy spoke eloquently about these conflicting needs.

I never really thought it would be this way. My life, that is. You see, I have an inordinate desire to be liked. Yet my life has been riddled with the pain and confusion of unintentionally creating enemies. I have been offered multiple opportunities to examine the question of how does one love one's enemies. As I walked into the unmarked land as a woman pastor, I learned to expect resistance. Hateful words and hostile actions have marked the trail.

Stereotypes and jumping to conclusions often muddy the interactions between people who sense difference. The tenacity of an ecumenical heart that embraces a vision to love can clean things up. Stefanie told this poignant story.

> Back in the mid '60s, when I had just professed my perpetual vows as a Benedictine sister, I had my first taste of public higher education and perhaps my first taste of religious diversity. I was in the process of moving to high school teaching, and I was spending the summer in double sessions to pick up the last couple of courses needed for certification.
>
> When I walked into the classroom at the local state college, I had no idea what lay ahead, but I was excited about the course and was finding this secular campus very interesting. The town was predominantly Catholic, so I wasn't too unusual in my traditional habit. I wasn't even aware that I was dressed differently. Remember, this was in the '60s.
>
> When I saw the teacher, my first impression was that he looked a lot like my older brother and like someone I should know. Then he saw me. His face turned to stone, but his eyes glared malevolently. I couldn't figure out what was happening. That continued throughout the next several weeks.
>
> This was a contemporary European literature class using several collections of short stories. It soon seemed to me that every author was anti-Catholic, anticlerical, anti-God, and the teacher was pounding the "anti" for all he was worth. I had an excellent background in literature from my Catholic college and from the reading my mother had guided as I was growing up, so I really enjoyed the class, even

though I quickly thought the "anti" boring, and I couldn't figure out why I was always called on to respond to the attacks on the Church.

As the summer moved on, the teacher's glares lessened, as did his antagonism. But I was still puzzled by his attitude. Surely it couldn't be directed at me! The course included a conference with the teacher, and for some reason, when I came for my conference, I brought the teacher some fresh chocolate chip cookies our cook had just made for me, and he gave me a red, ripe tomato from his garden. We had an excellent conference. The course ended happily, and I thanked the teacher for an enjoyable experience.

The next summer I was back for more courses and stopped by to see the teacher. This was when he told me that he had been raised a Catholic and learned to hate the Church and anyone associated with it in a professional way. When I walked into that room, he saw everything he hated there in me and was determined to hate me right back out of the room and the course. He did his best, but, as he said, "You kept coming back for more and were a good student besides."

This was the first time I had experienced anything like this, and it startled me. I thought I had seen hate in his face, but that it really was hate was sobering. After that we visited frequently, and I heard more of his story. It didn't take long for friendship to grow and for me to see him as one of the most believing atheists I could imagine.

Further thinking:

1. Share a challenging story that has shaped your faith.

2. What fears do you have about other traditions? How did they develop?

3. Talk about a story of grief and faith.

4. What are some of the barriers in your faith community to working with other churches?

Part II
Learning to Be Neighbors

Chapter 4
Listening to the Sages

*"Little children, let us love, not in word or speech,
but in truth and action. And by this we will know that we are
from the truth and will reassure our hearts before him whenever
our hearts condemn us; for God is greater than our hearts,
and he knows everything."*
1 John 3:18-20

Mentoring is important in nearly all areas of life. Big Brothers and Big Sisters bring children together with adults to form more than friendship. New teachers on all levels of education are paired with experienced teachers. Apprenticeships and internships are common in the business world. Mentoring might be deliberate or it might be accidental—or even providential. Ecumenism too has need of mentors. Persons who seem to have an affinity for ecumenism can look to their own lives and find that mentors, known in the flesh or through books or other media, have helped them, whether deliberately or unintentionally, to develop the virtues needed for ecumenical thought, interest, or engagement.

Robert never knew his mentor personally.

I have certainly been influenced by a multitude of persons in my ecumenical life, and I hope I never claim to be a self-made man. In the last ten years I have experienced great growth under able and grace-filled men and women of diverse backgrounds. But the mentor who is foremost in my mind is Thomas Merton.

Merton died in 1968, almost four years before I was born. Nonetheless, through teachers in seminary I was brought face to face with this man through his writings. Merton grew up without religious training, but was converted to Christianity when a graduate student at Columbia University. He later entered the Trappist monastery of Gethsemani in Kentucky and wrote prolifically until his death.

One of the virtues I have learned from Merton is integrity. I cannot face God or my neighbor, both of whom I want to love, unless the love that I offer is authentic. I have incorporated as an ecumenical virtue this pursuit of a holy or authentic life. My love for others cannot be conditioned on their subscribing to my own ideals, beliefs, and opinions.

I do not blindly accept others but spur them on to holiness of heart and life and to pursue the development of their own faith. Merton reminds me that the inauthentic life is really not worth living. My desire is to approach God with a pure heart and mind, and to avail myself of God's transforming love.

The integrity Robert has learned from Merton is a challenge. It calls for an authentic love that respects, welcomes, and encourages others. It asks that we hold our own beliefs and honor them while we encourage others to do the same within their traditions. It demands a momentary suspension of judgment for a reexamination of situations and of persons. Susan catches this in her reflections on Luke 7:36-50.

> The woman—a sinner, we are told—bathes Jesus' feet with her tears, dries them with her hair, and anoints them with the precious ointment in her alabaster jar. Jesus accepts the gesture and predicts that her story will be told in remembrance of her.
>
> The Pharisees, judgmental hosts, are compared to children sitting in the market place and calling to one another, "We played the flute for you, and you did not dance, we wailed, and you did not weep." They do not see that the guest becomes host in receiving the gift, that the host extends hospitality by receiving the gift.

So often when we give, we receive as well. Often our pleasure is in the giving, and we don't realize what we are receiving. There is a turnabout. In ecumenism too, we are enriched as we hope to enrich others—perhaps with a new or expanded understanding, with a deeper appreciation, with a new way of seeing things.

Tim, mentored by the Spirit, hears, sees, hopes, and believes anew.

> I am reminded of little Much Afraid who longs to journey into the mountains with the Gentle Shepherd *(Hind's Feet in High Places)*. Persistent abandonment is the key. God's sheep know his voice. Yet it is often easier to follow the herd than the Shepherd. Still, we have the Savior's promise that there will be one flock. I am greatly encouraged by this.
>
> As my hearing has sharpened, I find I have recognized more of God's people than ever before. Though

I am sure I have misidentified some and inadvertently excluded others, I know that God knows which sheep belong to him. I am willing to submit to his final determination.

I believe submitting to God's Spirit is the chief ecumenical virtue. It results in our being conformed to the image of God's Son. At the same time, the Spirit produces fruit in us in exact opposition to the divisive words of the flesh. I hope for Christian unity in this life; I am confident of it in the world to come.

Roberta, mentored by Philoxenus "across 1600 years, gender, language," also sees in a new way, nonjudgmentally.

On a particularly dreary day, surrounded by piles of books, I picked up thirteen ascetical homilies of Philoxenus of Mabbug. I opened to the middle of a homily talking about the need for monks (and all Christians by extension) to understand not to be judgmental about each other, because God looks at us with so much compassion. Then my world really did crack open. I was astounded that anyone would ever have thought such things. "If this is the case, everything in my life is going to have to change." I didn't know what it meant, but I knew my world had turned upside down.

Philoxenus was the start of everything for me: a sixth-century heretical bishop writing for monks in the Syrian desert—that was my conversion. The ability of that nonjudgmentalism to reach across 1600 years, gender, language—growing into a radical way of seeing God and ourselves in those nonjudgmental lives is an ecumenical virtue. Generosity might be a better term, though I haven't come up with something that really works.

While Roberta grapples with the nonjudgmentalism of a sixth-century monk, Patrick recognizes the wisdom of a sage a millennium and a half earlier, the medium of Endor in the story of King Saul, and learns about the "God Who Won't Give Up," the God to whom we are tightly bound.

You think you've hit bottom. You have been successfully practicing your profession for many years, when suddenly the government changes and the new leader outlaws people like you. Many have fled the country. Executions are rumored. You live in a remote area, and have managed to keep a small underground business going, but at any moment somebody could betray you to the police. Things can't get tougher than this.

But they can. Three men show up and ask you to do what you do. You suspect a trap: "Don't you know what the government has decreed? You're going to get me killed!" One of them swears that there won't be any punishment. Hesitantly, you agree to do the job. And as soon as you do it, you realize: The one who has asked you to do it is the one who has forbidden it.

The head of the government, faced with war, has found that the religious authorities can give him no guidance. They cannot tell him whether God is with him, or even what God wants him to do. He has asked his bodyguards to find for him somebody who does what you do. And, somehow, they know about you. They are in a tight spot: "If we tell him where to find one, he will know we haven't eliminated them all." But these are desperate times, and they have brought him to you.

This is the situation of the medium of Endor (1 Samuel 28), to whom King Saul comes on the eve of battle with the Philistines. She calls up the ghost of the prophet Samuel, who gives Saul the grim message that "the Lord has turned away from you and has become your adversary," and Saul will die the next day. The king, already weak from hunger, falls to the ground at the shock of this prophecy.

"The woman went up to Saul and, seeing how greatly disturbed he was, she said to him, 'Your handmaid listened to you; I took my life in my hands and heeded the request you made of me. So now you listen to me: Let me set before you a bit of food. Eat, and then you will have the strength to go on your way.'" Saul refuses, but eventually gives in to the urging of his bodyguards and the woman, and eats the fatted calf she kills and cooks. "Then they rose and left the same night."

Saul has only a few hours to live, but in this final despair the medium of Endor has offered him hospitality that speaks of a God whose care doesn't give up or give way. The woman he has outlawed serves him. The medium of Endor is an icon of the God who makes covenants, who speaks and listens: "Your handmaid listened to you; now you listen to me." This story reverses the perspective of Psalm 139, where we say to God, "Where can I go from your spirit? Or where can I flee from your presence?" In the medium of Endor I hear God saying to us and to the world: "Where can I go from your spirit? Or where can I flee from your presence? You are in my heart, so even my attempt to forget you or disown you binds me tighter to you."

We are also each other's mentors, opening each other's eyes to see in new ways. Even as we mentor, we are mentored, and perhaps when and where we least expect it.

Maggie learned this and was amazed. In her tradition icons are an indispensable part of worship. The icon is a sacred representation of Christ, the Mother of God, saints and angels, or even events of sacred history. It is an expression of revelation, "theology in visible form." Maggie could claim to be mentored by the icons she lived with daily. But in this instance, the mentoring was done not by the icon but by persons from other religious traditions and their appreciation of a specific icon.

> Within a day of the opening of our second session a large icon of Rublev's Old Testament Trinity, also known as the Hospitality of Abraham, was presiding serenely over our gathering.
>
> I am not quite sure how the specific decision came about to invite its presence, but it had to be some reference I made, since iconography is a very important part of my Orthodox tradition.
>
> I made an introduction to the group on iconographic elements and the role of this art in ritual and private devotion. But from then on I was amazed at the deeper meanings and spiritual insights that my Protestant and Pentecostal friends discovered in the icon. It spoke to them as clearly as it does to those in my church who are in the ambience of icons daily. It was a most amazing lesson to me that the sharing of traditions can enlarge and deepen each tradition. And we can make amends to each other by sharing what we have discovered in our separate journeys.

Stefanie picked up on what Maggie had to say in her presentation and took it a step beyond.

> Maggie says that what an icon tells us is this: "Be still and know that I am God." She says that an icon

is never signed with a name but with the words "done by the hand of the servant of God." In regard to our ecumenical work we might ask ourselves, "Is our work—is our being ecumenical 'beings'—done by the hand of the servant of God?" This also speaks to our need to remember who we are and who works in us. What I mean to say is that our ecumenical work cannot be self-promoting in any sense. We need to do it personally, heart to heart, figuratively touching the heart or the eyes or the ears of the other and letting them do the same for us, but we must always remember that we are servants of God and not God— that what we do is done by Jesus within us and not by ourselves alone.

Mentors are often found in our own families. While we might be aware of them from the start, it might also take reflection years later before we recognize fully how and what they have opened for us. Ina Dixon taught her great-granddaughter, Vera, not through words but through how she lived her daily life.

Thirty miles separated the hometowns of my parents. Thirty miles from the German Catholic Church of Saint Anthony to the Christian Church (Disciples of Christ) in Casey. That's how I saw the difference as a child. Saint Anthony's was huge, quiet, mysterious. The Latin language was familiar to me—the music and smells and bread and wine were the same as in my own parish. My mother's family had been coming here for a century.

On my father's side, the Christian Church of my great-grandmother, Ina Dixon, was simple, straightforward, and the services were in English. Except for the times the minister said, "Let us pray," we did not put our heads down, but rather looked out to our neighbor. At Communion time we passed the tray of wine glasses, with smiles to one another. My uncle Omar drank the grape juice as if it were from a shot glass. Of course I could not receive, at least when my mother was there. My grandmother Irene gave us quarters to put into the collection plate.

Ina Dixon taught me about ecumenism. She did not do so with deliberation but simply through the way she lived her life. I had been taught that only Catholics would go to heaven. I knew that simply could not be true. My great-grandmother could quote Scripture; her Bible was always within view. She took in strangers who were homeless, allowing them to sleep on beds put up in her kitchen. She loved me, her Catholic great-granddaughter. Everyone knew she was an especially holy person.

My father, who I believe loved God in his own way, did not go to church, but he thought his grandmother was a saint. Ina Dixon taught me to be open and curious about other traditions. She taught me to pray out loud—with spontaneity as she did before our huge feasts of homegrown vegetables spread out on her kitchen table.

I love Catholicism and my Catholic roots—it is where I learned to love God. I need also the Ina Dixon story. The Second Vatican Council may have allowed an openness between Catholic and Protestant traditions, but my great-grandmother's life did that for me first.

Just as we sometimes forget the importance of salt in giving us enjoyment of our food, so we often look for heroes and overlook the people who daily leave our lives

the better for having lived side by side with us. Stefanie's
time spent reflecting on a Scripture passage led her to
this insight.

> The salt of the earth and the light of the world (Mat-
> thew 5:13-16). These are common, ordinary meta-
> phors for the Christian. Neither salt nor light by
> itself is dramatic or romantic. But when we eat food
> without salt, we can't help but note the blandness.
> When we watch the light break through the clouds or
> brighten the darkness, we know beauty and awe. So
> too with our own lives: one who is the salt of the earth
> gives flavor to the lives of others; one who is the light
> of the world reflects for us the light and love of Christ.

> So often when we think of the lives of people whose
> example can spur us on, we think of big-name figures
> like Mother Teresa or Dorothy Day or Desmond Tutu.
> And then so often we say, "But I'm no Mother Teresa,"
> and settle for less than we could be. Maybe the prob-
> lem with holy celebrities is that as good as they might
> be, we have elevated them beyond our reach and so
> also have made their virtues seem unattainable for
> those of us who don't feel "big" enough.

> What makes good sense to me, then, is to look to the
> everyday people who sit quietly at our side, those
> salt-of-the-earth people who flavor our lives more
> than we realize because they are always there, al-
> ways faithful, struggling but enduring joyfully and
> quietly whatever might come. If virtues grow in rela-
> tionships and relationships flourish in community,
> whether family, parish, or religious, then these ordi-
> nary people rubbing shoulders with us are the ones
> who teach us the virtues of patience, gentleness,
> humility, commitment, generosity, appreciation, all
> leading to joy.

Joy comes from following Christ and embracing his teaching—both the cross and the resurrection. Joy is what lets the light of Christ shine through us to light up the world. And since virtues grow slowly and need intention to grow at all, the example of those around us all the time is our best support.

Granny Lindsay is just such an example. She might not have seen herself as an influential person, but her saltiness shows through her story and speaks to Nancy's heart.

When all else fails, remember Granny Lindsay. Granny Lindsay was known by everyone in our neighborhood. She lived to be over a hundred years old. Her house was only a few doors down from the church house where I served on the staff. When I needed a good dose of perspective, I walked down the street to see Granny. She had eyes that danced with life, even as her body edged toward death. Stories tumbled out of her as she told of picking cotton and going to bed with cracked and bleeding hands and feet.

One day I asked Granny, "What was the hardest time in your life?" I expected stories of poverty and prejudice from the racist soil of her heritage. Instead she told me this story.

"It was a just a couple of years ago when my sister Emma came to live with me. Emma was sick, and there was no one left in the family to take care of her but me. What could I do? Kin is kin. But it didn't take my heart but two or three days to be filled in every nook and cranny with resentment.

"She was the baby sister that my daddy loved best. Emma wasn't disciplined like the rest of us. The hickory stick never crossed her legs. She was spoiled through and through. The world revolved around Emma, while the rest of us spun around, spinning with resentment. Even as an adult, she was the queen of complaint. No one could do enough. When she came to live with me, she expected me to wait on her hand and foot. She would moan and groan if I asked her to help.

"Well, I couldn't stand it. My resentment grew till it smelled up the whole house like a mess of collards cooking. So I got down to some serious praying. Every morning I'd stir a pot of grits. Her favorite, mind you. As I stirred I asked God to remove this mountain of resentment. I stirred and I prayed. Day after day, I stirred and I prayed. Plenty of grits went down, until God finally set me free.

"You know what did it, child? I started feeling deep down that I couldn't love Emma. But I loved the someone who knew how to love her. And that was the beginning. I even got where I could laugh at myself and Emma—us two old women hobblin' around here tryin' to make do. Emma has eased up a bit, though she can still complain. But it doesn't stand in my way anymore. I just go on. I even have some love in my heart—a dab and a dash is a start. God is mighty big, child. God is mighty big."

The sages in our lives may be living or dead; they might even be characters in fiction. What we hear from others can be God's way of speaking to us, of influencing us for good, can change our lives. Are we listening?

Further thinking:

1. Reflect on what you listen to: music, news, neighborhood talk. How does what you hear affect your faith life?

2. Recall an individual who has influenced your life for the better.

3. In what ways can we mentor others in our daily living?

4. What do persons from Scripture teach you about forgiveness, hospitality, gratitude, humility, integrity, or virtues of your choosing?

Chapter 5

Living into Virtues

"Blessed are the poor in spirit, for theirs is the kingdom of heaven."
Matthew 5:3

Developing a virtue takes time and discipline. We aren't courageous, humble, grateful, or tolerant simply because we want to be. Virtues take steady, consistent practice. And just when we think we have a virtue mastered, something proves that we are no further ahead than when we first began. We have to "live into the virtues." They don't happen all at once. They come with conscious desire, perseverance, and the daily choices we make. Eventually virtues might even become second nature to us, although still just as deliberate and practiced as ever.

In Anwar el-Sadat, Patrick sees a vision and courage that move forward bravely beyond the status quo. Just as Sadat had to grow into his courage and learn to follow his imagination, we as individuals and as churches need to deliberately grow into courageous and imaginative solutions to what divides us.

"Next year in Jerusalem!" The closing words of the Passover Seder express the hope of every Jew. In 1976, apparently unbeknownst to anyone, this prayer was adopted by Anwar el-Sadat, President of Egypt. The following year he stunned the entire world by flying to Jerusalem to open peace talks with Israeli Prime Minister Menachem Begin.

I predict that historians many generations hence will highlight Sadat's going to Jerusalem as one of the defining moments of the twentieth century. It was an act of courage, and set in motion a train of events that ended in Sadat's assassination in 1981.

Acts of courage are not all that uncommon, however. Sadat's trip was that rarest of all political surprises: an act of imagination. Israel and its Arab neighbors were set against each other for what looked like forever. Just to maintain the status quo would have seemed a remarkable accomplishment.

But Sadat broke through all the assumptions, all the practicalities. He refused to accept reality as it had been handed to him. He imagined what couldn't be, and once he had done so, everything changed. Of course the Middle East is still a maelstrom, but Sadat made it clear that there is another way.

I keep waiting for church leaders to "do a Sadat." The reality is that we can't gather at the same table. But who says that's reality? It's possible to imagine otherwise, and then it could be so.

The term "Christian" carries great weight. Part of the weight is made up of expectations—the expectations of all of us who call ourselves Christian and the expectations of those who hear our proud claim to be Christian. Being Christian means reflecting Christ in how we live, being like him, practicing the virtues he lived.

Often, however, we are better at making our claims to being Christians than we are at living in a Christian manner. Our hypocrisy or our exclusiveness is apparent to all who see us. If we are honest, we recognize our exclusiveness for what it is and feel discomfort. For some, this insight comes at an early age. The grace found in this uncomfortable knowledge is the willingness to make the necessary efforts to be more truly Christian. This includes rejoicing in the faith of others. Mary Jane intuited this as a child but saw it lived by her mother.

> I was troubled, and even embarrassed, as a child that my church was named *The Christian Church*. What about those Baptist, Methodist, Presbyterian, Catholic, Church of Christ, Assemblies of God churches all over town—weren't they Christian? So why did we call our church *The Christian Church*? Later, I learned to refer to it as "The Christian Church Parenthesis Disciples of Christ Closed Parenthesis."
>
> Actually, the easiest response to "What church do you go to?" was "Presbyterian." After all, there was a Presbyterian church just across the street from my church, and we shared suppers and Sunday School programs sometimes. Or we share parking lots when something big was going on at one of the churches. I thought all these churches were the same anyway. For some reason they had just chosen different names.
>
> Somewhere along the way, the embarrassment about *The Christian Church* gave way to pride in its name. I had begun to think of it as a church that made no distinctions between Christians, and so, of course, that's why it had the name.
>
> That is the way it was for me. Never did I feel ours was the only way. It was one of many. And my grandmother and my mother, the wife and daughter of a Disciples minister, instilled this. They did this just by

the lives they led and by what they taught me and by what they didn't teach me. So did my father in his quiet life of compassion and generosity.

So, when I was living in New York, it was very easy for me to tell my mother in a telephone conversation that I had been to an Episcopal church a few times and liked the priest and that I even rather liked the ritual of it all. Her response was "That's wonderful." Not long after, Mother sent me a leather-bound Book of Common Prayer—"with love, Mother."

And it never entered my mind to make an issue of my husband-to-be's being a Catholic when I called my parents to say we were getting married. Mother had always been the one to whom we would talk about anything Church-related, and so when she was on the phone I said, "And by the way, he's Catholic." And her not surprising reply was, "Oh, I'm so glad!"

When Mother and my husband finally met each other, they were instantly simpatico. During our first visit to see my parents, Mother and my husband stayed at the dinner table long after everyone else had drifted away to more comfortable chairs. He was going through some of his criticisms of the Catholic Church that he had grown up in, as Mother listened patiently. And then she began to tell him all the fine things she saw in the Catholic Church. Later, he told me how that conversation had made him realize how grateful he was for his Catholic tradition.

Mother was basically an openhearted person, and so it would follow that she would be as open to Catholicism as she would be to other Protestant traditions. I think she had a special affinity for Catholicism because one of her very dear friends was Catholic. Their friendship was as strong as it was *because* they could share their different traditions. Their friendship always made me want to have a good Catholic friend, too.

What is in a word? Sometimes language can be descriptive in a way that catches our attention or gives special meaning. At other times language can be used to hide, to mislead, or to color reality. When this happens, dishonesty or pretentiousness creeps in. With his family, Dan shows us how to be aware and to beware of the pretentiousness we sometimes fall into.

> It began one day when I wondered aloud, "Why do they call expensive junk stores 'boutiques'? Why not just 'store'?" After that, when I'd hear a pretentious term, I'd say, "That gets me like boutique!"
>
> At family gatherings, we sometimes try to out-boutique one another, comparing the most "boutiquey words" we've heard. Even the grandchildren get into it. "What gets you like boutique, Grandpa?" Sometimes they use words that get me like boutique just to watch me cringe.
>
> It has become a family game that sharpens our alertness to pretentiousness.

After the insight comes the application. Of course it doesn't always work that smoothly. Often the insight surprises us because it turns our understandings or our expectations upside down. We need to look at reality or even at simple words in a new way. And then comes the challenge: we must live as the insight shows us. As Robert discovered, the false self must be shown up for what it is.

> *Blessed are the poor in spirit, for theirs is the kingdom of heaven* (Matthew 5:3). Nobody likes being poor.

But I would like to submit poverty as a virtue—a virtue of the ecumenical heart.

This first beatitude arrives boldly and unexpectedly. Against the beatitude, it is my expectation that what I should be doing instead is feeding my spirit, looking for occasions in which to nurture my soul, yearning for time with God, making myself rich in spirit. Should the beatitude not rather read, "Blessed are the rich in spirit, for theirs is the kingdom of heaven"?

Spiritual poverty arises when I realize that all that I take in, experientially and otherwise, amounts to nothing if it is only something I consume. I can read all the scriptural and devotional material I want, but the outcome is hollow if I do not bring my heart into fellowship with the Trinity. My life of spiritual poverty recognizes the impotence of my designs, of my plans, of my dreams and visions, when left to my own devices, even if these designs and plans are spiritual and are driven with good intentions. "Remember that you are dust, and to dust you will return."

What is to be avoided is a false spirituality, a spirituality that caters to what Thomas Merton calls the false self. I create my own false self when I refuse to allow God to operate in my life in transforming ways. When I make my own decisions about what is good for me and thereby refuse the full existence that God desires for me, I foster and preserve this false self. In other words, the true self is centered on God as God, but the false self tries to masquerade itself as God by creating its own ideas about living the holy life.

Merton writes, "In order to become myself I must cease to be what I thought I wanted to be." The true self that I really am exists beneath layers of inauthenticity to which I gravitate much too quickly.

Merton further explains: "To worship our false selves is to worship nothing. And the worship of nothing is hell." Fervent, authentic spirituality is found beyond the death of the counterfeit self.

The false self looks down on the true self as spiritually poor. True spirituality is not interested in playing the religious game or performing spiritual disciplines for what can be gained. Religion with integrity hopes only to gain Christ. The false self sees this as a meager goal. Why not impress friends and family along the way with your spiritual prowess? Why not be the object of adoration in your church community because you use Jesus-speak? Why not boast of the hours you spend every day visiting the elderly and ministering to the homeless? Simply to know Christ and the power of his resurrection seems a scant reward for the holy life.

"Blessed are the poor in spirit." May I always be found to be "poor in spirit," not trusting in my own strength but venturing myself with Christ and relying on God's grace.

Vera loved the stories the women in her family told. She not only learned her family's history but also learned the family's values and virtues. The stories became treasures that connected her with all the women in her family, but they did more than this. For Vera the stories became sources of both humor and hope, pointers to the virtues to be lived into.

Once a month or so my family made the three-hours' drive to my grandmother's home for a weekend visit. Once there, everyone dispersed. My father would go fishing or golfing and always beer drinking with my uncles. My brother, two sisters, and I would fly off to the various homes of our cousins. But what I perceived to be the heart of our family, the women, remained in the dining room of my grandmother's home. I would sit in a corner chair near the phone, hesitant to alert my cousins of our arrival, hoping to have more time in the presence and safety of these courageous and funny women.

The dining room was transformed into a beauty shop on Saturday afternoons. My Aunt Doris Jean would wash and pin curl my great-aunt Jeanie's and grandmother's hair. As she stood twisting strands of hair and securing them with bobby pins, my mother and her sisters would catch up on each other's lives. They would share funny stories about us kids, stories about husbands, past stories retold in new light, painful experiences which time had not yet healed, present worries, resolved worries. I especially loved it when they told stories on themselves. An embarrassing moment could be transformed into a funny story, and when told by the one who had experienced it, it became a great lesson in not taking yourself too seriously.

The tragic and the humorous story held equal attention in that room. One story told of my parents' wedding, held in the priest's home rather than the church because my father was not Catholic. It was related with sadness and some anger, as it had not only to do with Church teaching but also with who had money and who didn't.

I heard stories of the stresses of raising a family in the 1920s and '30s. My grandparents would send their six children off to confession on Saturday afternoons, not only to fulfill their obligation as good Catholic parents, but also to get a few moments of peace, only to have them back again soon after the nuns would chase that wild bunch out of church. Feeding hoboes on the back porch, taking in another child to feed and love, surviving the war years, caring for the older folk—these stories were better than anything I could see at the movies.

Sometimes everyone would talk at once, as we still do when we are together, but each understood this language which often escalated into fits of laughter. My grandmother would interject in her German way, "Ach, you silly girls!" and even my stern great-aunt would be smiling from her rocking chair in the other corner.

These stories, coming from the ones who it seemed both carried the burdens of the family and expressed its greatest joys, connected us and continue to do so. The laughter and storytelling took place in the midst of statues of the bleeding heart of Jesus, the sad-faced, open-armed Virgin Mary, the crucifix on the wall, and the prayer books on the dresser. There was nothing so serious that we could not still find reason to laugh together. Faith and humor—my family thrives on these as they both connect and give hope.

While we can all think of people who seem to have been born with certain virtues, we are also aware that growing into virtues takes a lifetime. It takes hard work and conscious choices over a long time, and requires the encouragement of a community.

Further thinking:

1. When have you been bold or imaginative in living your life of faith? When did you "do a Sadat"?

2. How do you personally live into the virtues? How do you encourage others?

3. When was an embarrassing moment turned into a moment of growth for you?

4. What can you do to encourage your church community to share the wisdom and virtue of other churches or traditions?

Chapter 6

Shaping Hearts

"Blessed are the pure in heart, for they will see God."
Matthew 5:8

The heart has always served as metaphor for the vessel of human feelings, emotions, and intentions. The "heart" contains our deepest thoughts and convictions. It holds the virtues. Or not. The metaphorical heart first appears in Genesis in the Noah story; the human heart, filled with evil thoughts, is juxtaposed to the grieving heart of God. A quick scan of Scripture reveals the human heart as upright, generous, discouraged, dull, proud and arrogant, humbled and exalted. The heart disclosed in Scripture holds wisdom, sorrow, anxiety, and treasures. It can rage, melt, bear witness, harden, backslide, and open.

We speak and meditate in the heart. The heart of a prophet beats wildly. The great command is to love "with all your heart." We are encouraged to "take heart" and not to "lose heart." In the New Testament the heart appears first in Matthew's Beatitudes: "Blessed are the pure in heart, for they shall see God." This complex vessel, which God sees into, can open our eyes to the heart of God and cause us to see anew.

"To what extent are the ecumenical virtues something we work on; to what extent does grace happen?" one person asked. To live with "an attitude of expectation" while simultaneously seeking and needing what others have to teach us is the stance of the ecumenical heart. "The heart is a gift to be discovered and cultivated": prayer, worship, mentors, suffering, discipline, years of seeking and expecting, as well as surprises which jar us loose—all precipitate the discovery and contribute to the shaping.

Tim observed the shaping of his mother's heart by marriage, illness, books, spiritual leaders, other faith traditions, the Spirit. As parents we may think we do most of the observing, but our children are being formed each day as they watch our lives and hearts taking shape.

> I suppose ecumenism is part of my family tradition, though until recently I had never really thought much about it. My German-Irish mother attended a Free Methodist church as a child. My dad's upscale (but poorer) family claimed both England and United Methodism as important parts of their heritage. When my parents married in 1955, they compromised, becoming members of a small Assemblies of God (Pentecostal) church. I was born a year later.

> Their decision was influenced, in part, by Oral Roberts. An Assemblies of God minister himself at the time, Roberts had a national reputation for his healing ministry. This attracted my parents. My mother was a nursing student, my dad a draftsman troubled by a long illness punctuated by various major surgeries. They sought healing for him at one of Roberts' crusades.

> My dad never received his healing, but my parents were impressed enough with Roberts to leave their Methodist churches and join the Assemblies of God.

Ironically, Roberts left the Assemblies of God shortly thereafter to become a Methodist minister. My mother settled into her new church with enthusiasm, teaching Sunday School and serving as church treasurer.

Yet for all her enthusiasm, my mother was long denied an experience she desired greatly: the Baptism of the Holy Spirit. She diligently attended church prayer meetings and state camp meetings. She read books by Toser, Moody, and Sherrill. She fasted for forty days, twice. She sought out spiritual leaders outside her new denomination, an unusual act at the time. We watched Rex Humbard on television and attended Kathryn Kuhlman services several times in Youngstown, Ohio.

My most vivid memory of her quest, though, is of sitting in a room, watching my mother praying in a circle with nuns in their habits and men with clerical collars. It was in Cambridge, Pennsylvania, a small town north of Pittsburgh, one of the many home-cell groups that sprang from the Catholic renewal at Duquesne University in the early sixties. The feature that made such an indelible imprint on my mind was that the room was filled with tobacco smoke. That was a shock! Smokers who spoke in tongues and prophesied! They were Catholic, no less. Douglas Weed would later record the renewal under a title that echoed my own surprise, *Father MacDonald Speaks in Tongues and Smokes a Pipe*, later reissued under the staid but more socially acceptable title, *Catholic Charismatics*.

I had thought speaking in tongues was a sign of Spirit baptism, awarded to those who had progressed well beyond salvation to a life of holiness and doctrinal purity. Now, I was hoist on my own petard. Could

Catholics possibly be saved? I was taught that they thought everybody else was going to hell, so, of course, we returned the thought in kind. Could God possibly be so blind? Could I have been so wrong?

For hearts to be transformed, "some experience must break the pattern, the rhythm, of the center of one's life, thereby repositioning the center, 'the heart' of one's values, expectations, assumptions, commitments, loyalties," Elena wrote. Stefanie resisted the "repositioning" which resulted from the changes in the rhythm of her parents' lives, but was eventually able to see the challenge as a grace.

> When I entered the monastery in 1960, I was the first in my family to move from home and really be gone. Twenty-five years later, it became clear that Mom and Dad could no longer live safely in our home with no family member nearby to look out for them. A retirement place was opening near me, 120 miles from our hometown, and they moved there. That was when it suddenly hit me: my parents were now *in my back yard* and I would forever be responsible for them.

> In the beginning it didn't mean much. But before long that changed as Mom became more crippled from her multiple sclerosis, and there were things Dad couldn't manage, or didn't feel up to doing. Each year brought more and more responsibility as their diminishment increased.

> It was a challenge from the start. I loved my parents and thought they deserved the best care—better than anything I could offer. I wanted to be there for them, but I felt selfish and at times thought I shouldn't have to bear all the responsibility. And then came—take

your pick here—the Voice, the "slap of conscious-
ness," the epiphany, the "stroke of grace."

I was on my way to see my parents one Saturday after-
noon, talking to myself. Suddenly, as I listened to
myself, it struck me that I had developed a mantra
that went like this: "My heart isn't in this! I don't
want to do this!" Just as this registered in my brain, I
heard the voice: *Then put your heart into this.* That
voice was so loud and clear that I heard an echo in
the car, and I had goose bumps. I knew what I had to
do. If I thought they deserved better, then the only
way it would be better for them was if I listened to
that voice and put my heart into my being with them.

That moment of grace has been far-reaching. I began
to see more clearly what I was doing and how I had
to change. I didn't stop to analyze it, and I didn't have
a complete, once-and-for-all conversion, alas, but I
had a beginning. It changed how I related to Mom
and Dad, and most of the time it made things better.
I came to see in a new way the gift my parents were
for me.

Since then, whenever things get tough, I remind myself to "put some heart into it." This has a way of
working a change. "To will one thing," a friend of mine
says, is how Søren Kierkegaard explains purity of
heart. Putting my heart into what I am doing is willing one thing. Isn't it also a starting point for developing an ecumenical outlook—putting our heart into
our relationships with people of all traditions?

Crisis is not the only impetus for change. When Robert
was a child, his judgment and heart melted, and religious
smugness gave way to sharing and love when his friend,
Shawn, surprised him and shaped his heart.

The church where I grew up held frequent Sunday School attendance drives, offering us grade-schoolers incentives such as sweets and toys to bring our friends to church. We received extra points for bringing our Bible, memorizing designated verses, and contributing to the offering, but the big scores were gained by bringing visitors.

I was a shy, quiet eight-year-old, confronted with the demands of this attendance drive. I always brought my Bible, had no problem memorizing the special verses, and usually had a coin or two for the offering plate. But if I wanted to get anywhere in the contest at church, I had to get my friends to church. More ominous, before I could get them to come, I had to ask. And for a timid boy, this was a lot to expect.

Shawn used to pick on me when I was smaller, but by the third grade we were good friends. To my knowledge neither Shawn nor his parents went to church with any regularity, so he seemed a likely candidate to be my visitor. And if he declined my invitation to come to church, I would probably not lose face with him.

One day as we were shooting baskets in my driveway I asked if he was interested in coming to church with me that Sunday. He declined the invitation, assuring me that he already attended a Lutheran church in town. I did not believe him. He had never talked of church involvement in the past. I didn't know how to "prove" whether he attended church or not until I had a brainstorm.

The only thing that I knew other churches knew was the Lord's Prayer. I asked him if he knew it, and he did. There on the driveway, in the middle of shooting baskets, Shawn and I prayed the Lord's Prayer together,

and we sang "Jesus Loves Me." It was my first ecumenical experience.

Some people seem to be natural ecumenists, not only
finding it easy to break down barriers, but rarely seeing
them in the first place. Breathing the air of these folks, or
sharing an office with one, can gently shape a heart for
ecumenism. Vera's friend, Tom, did this for her in his life
and in his death. Because Tom was an organ donor, his
heart extended the life of a stranger, but his friends and
community continue to be shaped by his metaphorical
heart.

> I remember a day when Tom Jolly wore three beepers.
> Tom Jolly. The name fit. Short, bearded, a little round
> with a laugh you could hear all over the hospital cafe-
> teria. I shared an office with Tom at my first place of
> work as a hospital chaplain. From him I learned about
> connectedness. It was as if bridges just grew right out
> of Tom over him into all kinds of territory.
>
> It was not in Tom's job description to visit and have
> coffee at the nurses' stations each day, but he viewed
> that as an important part of his work—saying hello,
> getting the scoop, hearing the stories of our workers,
> making them feel as if they were a part of the whole,
> connecting one station and floor and person to an-
> other with invisible connecting dots like in a *Family
> Circus* cartoon.
>
> Tom would sit in his office in the early morning, call-
> ing new clergy and old to say hello, ask about family,
> invite to a meeting or to lunch. In addition to work-
> ing full-time at the hospital, he pastored a Christian
> church in a small town thirty miles away. Those folks
> would call him on his beeper also. He was almost al-
> ways and everywhere reachable. The hospital was a

perfect place for Tom; not only did it provide him with beepers, but it also provided a center for his ecumenical spirit and work.

Tom fell one Saturday evening while playing tennis with his son and died nine days later of a brain injury. Surprising things happened during those nine days and in the weeks to follow as Tom again connected us.

Area clergy gathered around his bed while a Catholic woman anointed him. The rabbi spoke about Tom's hospitality on a Saturday morning in a Disciples church. A tough-talking, gun-wielding hospital security guard wrote a poem and read it at a standing-room-only memorial service in the hospital chapel.

The hospital received enough money in his memory to create a room for study and rest in the back of the chapel. One beautiful fall evening many of us gathered to dedicate that room to Tom. It was blessed by a Jew, a Muslim, a Catholic, a Disciple, and a Pentecostal. Tom's picture smiles over those who enter that room to read, pray, or rest. I sometimes go to that room when I am feeling disconnected—there is a bridge there.

There are those who walk ahead of us and pave the way. Father Joe's courage in sharing his own struggle and story gave Carol strength and hope to continue her own journey of spiritual growth.

His name was Joe, and he was an alcoholic, a very wise alcoholic, a man of God who had walked the road I had before me. Joe shared his experience, strength, and hope. I wasn't alone. Someone else had been there. Fortunately, I never felt totally separated from God, but I thought that I had turned my life over to God (Step Three). I was still alcoholic.

Had God failed? Impossible thought! The alternative was my own failure and a load of guilt beyond bearing.

As we sat around those tables, Joe discussed his own disease and the process of his recovery in such a way that my struggles were addressed. I had never doubted that God could. Joe nudged me along the path to belief that God would. Belief leads to faith, faith to trust, trust to expectation. The practicing alcoholic cannot mature spiritually. I had become stuck somewhere before faith led to trust. How good it was to hear Joe's message. I didn't need to stay stuck. In fact, I had to grow or stagnate and die.

Joe prompted me to ask questions. Does my understanding of God make a difference in the way I live my life? Does my relationship with God affect my relationships with others? How? Who is in the family? Joe helped me realize that I am the only one who can answer such questions. I have the tools to find the answers.

In Maggie's story, the curiosity and persistence of a child drawn to the enticing smells and love of a community is a blessing to both. The tradition shaped the child and in turn was shaped.

It is a tradition in Orthodox churches to share an Agape meal following the liturgy. Some of the larger churches offer coffee and sweet rolls, but smaller communities have a real honest-to-goodness meal prepared by parishioners.

At one of these smaller communities, located in a poorer neighborhood of the city, a young African American, enticed by cooking smells, wandered in and was invited to stay and share in the Agape meal.

He then appeared quite regularly on Sunday mornings and occasionally brought his friends.

He began arriving early enough to check out what was going on in the nave and sanctuary where the liturgy was ending. He was intrigued and particularly envious of the altar boys garbed in their vestments with crossed stole.

Over a period of time he became a regular church attendee and asked the priest if he could participate fully as a member. The priest, a bit perplexed because of the young fellow's age, sought counsel with the bishop. The answer came that, if there was parental approval and the young man was cognizant of the faith to the best of his young ability, it would be a valid conversion. The young African American is now a member—and an altar boy.

Our stories describe numerous ways in which the virtues have been discovered and nurtured within ourselves, but they also point toward an urgent need for the nurturing of hearts in the church and the culture we live in. Dan recognizes the urgency and importance of intentionally shaping hearts. "What we are working on is the heart of what it means to be Christian," he says. "Develop a common character, and then we can deal with the doctrinal differences." Dan addresses the issue of clergy formation—examining the heart of the ministerial candidate and providing experiences and programs that shape it. His message reaches beyond clergy, as the virtues he describes can reduce conflict, bitterness, and stresses in our communities and world.

The candidate stood nervously before the presbytery after reading the theological formulas he had offered as his statement of faith. He waited for questions from the floor, most of which turned out to be theological formulas also. Few asked how he had come to decide on ministry or what had happened to him on the way. The dry exercise came to a merciful end with a motion to "arrest the examination, excuse the candidate, and proceed to discussion and vote on his ordination."

It's hard to assess readiness for ministry, and it's hard to know how to help candidates prepare. Sound theology is essential, but its usefulness in ministry depends on coming to terms with life and self, Church and culture—and God in the total mix. In a day when "the once-and-future Church," "the disestablishment of the Church," "the post-Christian era," and "the awkward Church" describe our predicament, theology doesn't even make sense without a realistic grasp of context.

The criteria we use today have to do with doctrinal matters, the quality of a candidate's experience, and personal psychological factors. We get what information we can from statements of faith, personal testimony, reference checks, and psychological tests. We have no way in public to inquire into *the* fundamental tool of ministry, which is the minister's soul. The recent addition of homosexual activity as a negative criterion has done nothing to soften our problem, for it puts us no closer to the heart of the matter or to the heart of the candidate.

Pastoral ministry is under increasing stress and disquiet, now intensified by issues that cannot be resolved biblically, doctrinally, historically, legislatively, or judicially. An alarming number of ministers and congregations are breaking under the demands, ambiguities, and stresses.

Our essential problem, however, has to do not with tools but with ministry. We lack a consensus about what constitutes effective ministry today, which, in my experience, is a mysterious and complex relationship between three selves—the self of the minister, the self of the one or ones ministered to, and the self of God—in which something happens to connect the now and the eternal in a life-changing way. We could get away with ignoring the self's part in ministry when there was a consensus and broad support for the minister's role. The internals are crucial now, however, because the externals are confused.

Is there a paradigm that can serve us? Yes. It comes from the realm of virtues, which can, when shaped to the demands of ministry, give us access to the soul-characteristics that fit a person for this mysterious and complex enterprise: what it takes to ready a self for a ministry that is conducive to personal, congregational, and community health.

What virtues ready a person for an ecumenical heart?—by which I don't mean just a heart that loves to sit in ecumenical councils, but one centered in God and open to diversity. Here is a list of such virtues:

Realism which unmasks the illusions of a deceived heart

Freedom which liberates from the illusion that I own either my heart or its source

Gratitude which accepts and affirms all the sources that have nurtured me, including my repressive Church tradition

Confidence-in-grace which can withstand the frantic and escalating repressiveness of legalism

Hopefulness which celebrates life within a messy and contentious world

Humility which knows how to join with other ecumenical hearts, from whatever context or tradition

Integrity which can withstand the meanness of contemporary Church and civic politics

Love which seeks ways to relate to threatening enemies

Conversion which is continually open to the Gospel

Forfeit of absolutes which invites others to surrender their absolutes

Risk which invites others to surrender the illusion of security

Rootedness which offers conviction-amid-diversity to an aimless age

A *sense of incompleteness* which seeks wholeness in another

A *yearning* which is open to the yearnings of others.

Virtues for an ecumenical heart can grow from the wreckage of a broken heart and can transform the suffering of a chastened heart. They are both given and achieved, caught and taught, natural and nurtured, and we know them when we see them, although many are experienced and never recognized. Though innate, they are capable of cultivation, and therefore we can understand, teach, encourage, cultivate, honor, and celebrate them.

Further thinking:

1. Imagine how your heart would need to change to be more open to others.

2. Who have you learned from about reaching out to others? How did they teach you?

3. How can an ecumenical heart change your daily life and influence the world in which you live, i.e., your work, politics, community organizations, etc.?

4. Share a story of when your heart was "repositioned."

Part III
Living As Neighbors

Chapter 7
Journeying Together

"Lord, you have been our dwelling place in all generations.
Before the mountains were brought forth,
or ever you had formed the earth and the world,
from everlasting to everlasting you are God."
Psalm 90:1-2

An intergenerational quality to the ecumenical heart transcends limits that are often posed by those who judge the contributions of others. Stories about youth and young adults repeatedly moved us to a renewed sense of hope. The ecumenical heart welcomes the insights of youth, even though—or because—sometimes those insights are subversive. Brian remembers that at a youth gathering, where multiple clergy had been invited to offer the Eucharist simultaneously, students refused to go to their designated stations and crossed the lines to gather at altars outside of their own traditions.

Alva, many years ago, was part of an initiative that captured the forward-looking vision of youth and young adults.

As a teen in Jamaica, Queens, New York, I led a group called "The Seekers." Our advisors were seminarians from Union Theological Seminary. Denomination-ally we were United Methodist, Presbyterian, and Episcopalian. Ethnically we were black and white, though predominately black. We were male and fe-male. Most important, we were good friends.

It was the late '60s and we were seeking a place to "hang out," socialize, listen to our music—loud of course—dance, and just be together: a safe place to have fun.

After the prerequisite planning, The Seekers launched a combination discotheque and coffee house in the fellowship hall of the Presbyterian Church. Open on Saturday nights, the disco had the whole nine yards—live music, go-go dancers, and strobe lights. Our group of teens auditioned bands and dancers, created decorations including several seven-foot go-go cages, recruited volunteer workers, purchased the refreshments to be sold, managed the money, and cleaned up each night so that the fellowship hall was ready for church the next morning.

For 50-cents' admission, young people could dance and simply enjoy themselves. Or they could visit the coffee house in the basement where jazz, folk music, or poetry reading were served with coffee, Coke, and doughnuts.

As youth who believed that we could do anything, we were not surprised that we were very successful. The adults, however, were quite amazed. With limited advertising—we distributed flyers in the local high schools—we attracted overflow crowds week after week, a testimony to the need for a place for teens to safely hang out. The occasional lost coat was the ex-tent of "incidents"—to the astonishment of local law enforcement.

Looking back, it's not hard to see the many virtues exhibited: inclusiveness, boldness, hospitality, openness, commitment, celebration. Surprise? Not for Seekers. Perhaps the ecumenical heart is young!

The ritual life of communities often affords the opportunity for differing traditions to worship side by side. Even though we shape liturgy, liturgy shapes the community, too. The need to journey together with honesty and clarity helps explain why Dan prefers burying to marrying.

> I was fifty-four when I began my first typical Presbyterian pastorate. One reason it was typical was the many weddings and funerals which came our way. I knew how to do them but had never done so many. The cumulative experience took some getting used to.
>
> I surprised myself one day when I said to a parishioner who asked about funerals, "I'd do a funeral any day, rather than a wedding." "Why?" "Most weddings sap energy; most funerals generate energy! A wedding is a social event, and no matter how hard I work—and it's a lot of work—most of the time I contribute nothing more than an appendage. Funerals, on the other hand, are spiritual events. People are focused not on how they look but on how they feel, on the deceased, on one another. They're at life's edge, available for new meanings and God's surprising presence. Weddings rarely feel like ministry; funerals usually do."

The ecumenical heart recognizes integrity of experience and truth-telling. Whether in a discussion of funerals or the shape of community, there are bedrock values inherent in stories, values that speak profoundly about our life together. Gary writes:

Although we might be born with a native capacity for them, virtues must be cultivated in order to make them strong, full, habitual. Indeed, in cultivating them, we increase our capacity for them, as well as our ability to act out of them. I believe our most deeply held intellectual beliefs are rooted in—or at least tied to—deep, emotionally charged experiences and perceptions.

I've drummed on how important the experiences of dislocation and homelessness are for me, as well as the desire for home and welcome and belonging. Home-building, both spiritual and physical, finding and creating welcoming space, building and receiving community for myself and others—these virtues flow out of my needs and nurture the virtues necessary for the important heart work.

The community I seek as an ecumenical Christian will cultivate virtues that allow diverse people to flourish together without all becoming like me or like my community. If virtues flow from a community's understanding of what is good, in order for me to speak of the ecumenical heart I must reflect on the nature of Christian community and its conception of the good. Then I can figure out how we journey—together.

It is true that how we picture ecumenism is as much about vision as it is about practice. It is as much about agreements as it is about action. It happens in theological conversations and around coffee pots. Brian speaks about an experience that transcends its particular truth.

The first snapshot appeared in the mail. Crumpled, marked, and damaged, it was difficult to see what was there anymore. Someone, somewhere saw me in the picture, guessed that it was mine. It was found fifty miles away from my home. Tornadoes displace a worldview in seconds.

Months have passed. The funeral pall continues. Rehearsal of the catastrophe happens every day. The language is of loss and grief. The days are filled with disorientation and confusion. We think that the end is around the corner, but all we discover are more buildings destroyed, more lives displaced, more futures seem tenuous.

Recounting the stories reminds me that we are not the only ones to experience such challenges. Daily news reports echo the disasters happening around the world. The ravages touch each of us.

And yet, I'm also reminded that our little world has been changed and how I picture what I value has also changed.

The liturgy has been sustaining. Having space to be with each other is more crucial than I ever imagined. On Palm Sunday, we processed to the barren valley, and like splendid palm branches, we knew that we had been strewn into the path of Our Lord.

On Good Friday, we planted the first tree of life, an awesome mystery, for in its death and burial we were reborn. Together we cast dirt on the encased roots as they were lowered into the earth tomb.

We watered it. We left it there, shadowed and protected by the oldest remaining tree on campus.

Resurrection Vigil kindled a fire to remember the Eternal Flame that was found burning in the chapel skeleton immediately after the winds. It remained there, suspended from the ceiling during those first days following the storm, and continues to remind us that the doors will always be open, and the light will always be burning, as we search for the remnants of home.

All of these events were welcoming and hospitable to people who find themselves inside or outside of denomination, Church, and tradition. We were able to do this, I think, because Christ Chapel at Gustavus, the college where I serve, has been a house with many rooms for belief. In the pew are Roman Catholic and Lutheran hymnals. Jewish, Buddhist, and Muslim believers have joined Christians in speaking during daily worship.

Other pictures have emerged. They have marked my memory indelibly. The first gift to arrive came from the Catholic Church. The diocese heard that I had lost my home and sent money to begin the rebuilding process. Me, a Lutheran. They sent more than money, they sent hope.

Since Saint Peter's Catholic Church had to be closed, First Lutheran welcomed them to use the facility, and shared worship on Maundy Thursday and the Vigil of Easter. Shared preaching, shared music, shared Eucharist, emergency situation.

It is easier to meet each other in our grief than it is in our doctrinal agreement.

Students, faculty, and staff from colleges around the Midwest appeared on campus immediately for assistance. Offers came from around the country. Denominational affiliation provided the resources so that this wide net of Christian assistance could find its way to our doors.

Meals were shared where electricity was working. People opened up their homes for those without.

There was no need for the preliminary conversations and checking each other out. We didn't have time to talk about our differences in belief. We moved quickly beyond these "niceties" to meeting each other's real needs.

Some have said that this storm is the worst to have faced any college or university in the United States. We have said that the act of God has been the generosity of the human spirit which has been given so freely. I've begun to expand how I picture the relationship and value of denominations and also our ability to transcend their limits and share their inherent gifts.

Vera's story shows that ecumenical hearts welcome others without regard for the categories that often impede relationship. After ten years working as a hospice chaplain, she still experiences awe in meeting a new patient and family.

As I approach their home, I think of the whole life I am about to meet. Not just a life living in the present, but someone reflecting on an entire life. Dying individuals have an urgent need to ask the big questions. "Who have I been?" "Whom have I loved and who has loved me?" "Has my life made a difference?"

They are also thinking about their future—not about what their next degree will be or where they will vacation next summer, but rather, "Will my death be peaceful?" "Will my family be okay?" "Have I been good enough?" "Will God be waiting for me?" Spiritual assessment is an awesome thing. Reflection on these questions unfolds throughout our relationship, but what I am often met with as I arrive with my anxiety is hospitality.

Betty lives by herself in a simple, comfortable, and inviting home. She lets me in the door saying, "Honey, from now on just come in, in case I don't hear you." Her recent story includes a divorce, a terminal illness, a grandchild who was in a serious accident, and five children whom she doesn't want to burden with her troubles.

I ask and discover that she is a Southern Baptist. She never even asks about my tradition but is completely open to my presence. She cries and apologizes for crying. At some point she gets up, her long oxygen tube trailing behind her, to fix us a cup of tea. "I don't dare ask God for healing," she says, "because he has already blessed me so much."

My own life often feels so incomplete. I have not finished my master's degree. I am forty-four and we have never owned a home. Too many unfinished projects. I'm never quite the mother I think I should be. My own faith tradition as a Catholic often feels so lacking. I never give enough time to my prayer life. Betty has let go of all that and has room for hospitality—an awareness of being blessed. I pray with her—and she prays for me. Sometime we get a glimpse of completeness.

And Vera, her mind full of the sounds coming from her teenaged son's boom box, finds her own thoughts responding to that rhythm and beat.

An Ecumenical Rap

"Just a closer walk with thee,
Grant it Jesus if you please.
Daily walking close with thee,
Let it be, Dear Lord, let it be."

I'm walking with God in the morning sun.
I take a look around,
I'm not the only one.
All kinds of people out to get a fresh start
Walking—it's good for the heart.

Criss-crossing the street I think of days of old
When to walk on the other side
was wrong we were told.
But when you're ecumenical—
You've got to be bold.

Who are my people on this long, hilly walk?
Are they the Catholics in my own church,
the Baptists down the block?
Pentecostals, Lutherans—or Swede?
How many roads to heaven do God's children really need?

We're mighty comfy in our own church, in our own private seat.
Familiar faces, prayers, doctrine may make us feel complete.
But a message of the Gospel is to
"Get up and walk!"
Jesus could have skipped the cross
had he only talked the talk.

He didn't stay within the temple,
but he walked among the poor.
He stepped up onto the mountain
and strolled along the shore.
He took water from the foreigner, preached love of enemy.
And when his friends became afraid—
he walked across the sea.

Some have been hurt by their own denomination—
hierarchy, patriarchy,
dislocation, alienation,
disregarded, discarded;
Stepped on, stepped over—told to take a hike.
No girls or gays allowed to preach—
Don't step up to the mike.

The story of the Savior is one of being homeless.
There was no room in the inn,
no welcome home from kin.
His loss led him out to the edge;
he taught forgiveness from the ledge.
Inside our church we're not complete;
We must step out—the stranger meet.

It's not hard to imagine a new diversity,
which doesn't focus on our doctrine, but is rooted in humility.
Don't let religiosity suppress your curiosity.
Step over to your neighbor's church—
receive some hospitality.

Bring along your story, but be prepared to listen.
Tell it for the glory, but observe what you've been missing.
Be surprised by words and songs that mend and open hearts.
Sharing wine may be taboo;
A cup of coffee just may do.
See where walking can lead to?

Cross the lines, then improvise; enter into conversation.
An ecumenical rap—it just may fill the gap.
An ecumenical rap—it makes your feet want to tap.
So tap out the door and move across the street.
Feel your ecumenical heart—
It has a good, strong beat.

Ecumenism—it's a beautiful word.
Ecumenical—it doesn't mean that we're identical.
We don't have to think alike
or worship God the same.
But tolerate. Celebrate. And praise God's holy name.

I'm walking in the evening shade,
giving thanks for this world which our God has made.
I take a look around—I'm not alone.
I'm walking with friends . . .
We're searching for home.

Further thinking:

1. Who are companions on your faith journey from outside of your faith tradition? How are they helpful?

2. Visit a neighbor's church with your neighbor.

3. What are other places in your neighborhood for nurturing ecumenical hearts?

4. Attend a worship service to celebrate cooperative ministry in your community. If there is no ecumenical service, start one.

Chapter 8

Standing in Faith

" . . . God is light and in him there is no darkness at all.
If we say that we have fellowship with him while we are
walking in darkness, we lie and do not do what is true;
but if we walk in the light as he himself is in the light,
we have fellowship with one another . . ."
1 John 1:5b-7a

Process, movement, change—all these are necessary to make an ecumenical heart. But at some point we have to stand—not stock-still, nor rigid, but rooted and grounded. The stories of positions taken, stands made, are not static and pedantic. They stir reflection, conversation, and action.

Curt asks, "What if I am going to live?"

Diagnosed with testicular cancer at age twenty-three, I had surgery and radiation treatments. The doctors felt confident they had cured the cancer but would only commit that, if I lived five years, I had a 95 percent chance of normal life expectancy. They offered no odds on the first five years.

I thought I was going to die soon. A general meltdown of my life occurred. My wife of five years agreed to a divorce. My employer, a bank in Boston, asked me to resign my position as a lending officer. The cancer, divorce, and job loss occurred in less than two years.

I told my oncologist what was happening with my life. He referred me to a psychiatrist who, after three brief sessions, asked, "What do you want to do with the rest of your life?" When I told him I wanted to travel, he told me about a friend who was traveling around on $5.00 per day, and said I should hit the road.

I did, and traveled from Mexico to Canada over the course of ten months, during which I had numerous opportunities to think about my life. It seems my largest concern was, "If God exists, why is my life like this?" I had reached a point where I couldn't see any evidence of the existence of God.

Driving over Raton Pass in New Mexico, I boldly told God that if he existed he would have to give me a sign. I immediately saw a small flash, a spot in front of the windshield. It looked like it could have been a bug, but there was no bug there. I said to God, "If that was the sign, it needs to be better."

Shortly thereafter, I saw a line in front of the windshield, a two-dimensional feature as opposed to the spot. It was fleeting, and again I said to God, "If that is the sign, it's not clear enough. It's got to be better."

As I drove along over the pass, I looked up into the sky and the clouds above me had formed perfect letters, G - O - D. "God, that is clear enough for me."

Until that time, I had been traveling around, seeing sights, wondering when I was going to die. After the vision of God's name I began to think, "What am I going to do if I happen to live?" I didn't have a plan for that contingency, but I knew I needed to develop one.

Eventually, I moved back to my home town, Kansas City. I abandoned banking, the field I was educated for, and went into the business I thought would be the most fun possible: real estate management. The job turned out to be everything I hoped for and more, preparing me to run my own real estate investment business that has also been more than I hoped for.

Besides business, did I ever find out what I was supposed to do with the rest of my life? No, but it continues to evolve each day.

God blessed me with a wife who supports me in taking large risks with our livelihood, and those risks have put us in a good financial position. She has recently left her job of eleven years with a large pharmaceutical firm, to pursue a master's degree in counseling psychology. We have made a decision to move to San Diego, our favorite city, when she graduates. I am restructuring our real estate investments and my business so that I will work part-time. I feel strongly that God has a plan for me in San Diego, but I don't have any idea what it is.

What am I going to do if I live? I don't know, but I do know that every day God will disclose enough to keep me busy for the day.

Susan sees virtues flowering when we really encounter one another.

Why do we tell stories to get at the virtues? I believe that theologian Richard Gula gets it right when he almost equates our stories with our identity: the stories we tell shape our vision, our vision forms our character, our actions flow from our character, and how we act with one another depends more on how we see than on rules. The question we're really discussing is not, "What ought I to do?" but "What do I see?"

When we tell stories, we are sharing our visions. When we listen to another, we glimpse that person's way of being in the world. Telling and hearing stories broadens our perspective, lets us see other possibilities. We enter into a wider community by expanding the circle of our world. We see more.

An ecumenical heart is really a way of being moral in the world. It's about loving people different from ourselves. It's about seeing from more than our own perspective, our own tradition. An ecumenical heart is an attribute of character. This means it's more than tolerance. It's positive appreciation. And it's more than appreciation at a distance. It's walking in another's footsteps for even a short distance, seeing what they see. Openness, capacity for dialogue, nondefensiveness, transparency—these are virtues for an ecumenical heart, one that can embrace the other, learn from the other, and value the other.

An ecumenical heart certainly has to do with more than formal Church unity (although such unity is surely not simple). The formal dialogues must go on, but common action, prayer together, being in one another's company—these can't wait, and without such living together, all the thinking together will come to nothing. An ecumenical heart enables us to come into communion with another. Formal and visible unity, the goal of the formal dialogues, can be finally achieved only by ecumenical hearts. And an ecumenical heart requires conversion, turning from a focus on the self, whether this be my own self or my tradition, so that I may gaze not only on the other, but also *with* the other.

Our stories suggest that none of us here set out consciously to develop an ecumenical heart. But some degree of homelessness or displacement figures prominently in many of our stories. This does not seem accidental to the journey that has brought us to our encounter with ecumenism.

An ecumenical heart is a grace, something that we do not shape as much as it shapes us. It is born out of wrenching and pain—whether rejection, dislocation, or just plain emptiness—that none of us would have originally chosen. We were blasted out of comfort, out of the known and the sure, into ambiguity, change, and dialogue. Would we have embarked on this journey had the status quo been an option? And even the stories that do not include major trauma tell of changes in attitude, of a shift from inherited suspicion, distance, and prejudice to unfamiliar trust and openness.

What is the discipline that nurtures an ecumenical heart? For starters, listening, and the willingness to befriend. Both listening and friendship require fidelity, patience, time, forgiveness. I have often felt judgment melting as I got to know someone better. This knowledge usually comes when we are vulnerable to each other as persons, shedding identities dictated by tradition. By vulnerable, I don't mean doormat, and I'm not advocating psychological dumping. I mean transparency, being authentic and honest, claiming personal ownership, not hiding behind rules and roles.

Here's a story. A friend of mine, a Sister of Mercy of Irish and Italian descent, had a brother, Nick, who had died of AIDS the previous year. Her father gave her his credit card and told her to take the family out to dinner on him. She invited me to come along. Seated around the table were my friend Pat and I, both members of religious communities; one of her brothers who had left his job and moved to San Francisco to take care of Nick in his illness; this brother's live-in girlfriend; Nick's partner, an architect who, based on his experience of caring for Nick, was quitting his job in the fall to go back to school to become a nurse; and Allen, a second brother who was then HIV-positive and who died about a year later.

Companion means "one who breaks bread with." The companionship that evening transcended sexual orientation, moral issues, even the grief and emotional exhaustion experienced by that family in the ordeal of Nick's illness and death. We did not dwell on the grimness of the past or Allen's ominous future, but sat in the companionship of the present moment. That moment was certainly deepened by the love shared and the bonds created by common suffering. Nick's death had profoundly changed lives—careers were abandoned and changed for service to a brother. The great Italian feast, gift of Pat's father's generosity, was a fitting setting for the greater liberality shown by their love and service of one another.

This experience typifies what is meant by both the Eucharist and an ecumenical heart. It was a sharing in communion, a transcendence of boundaries and judgment, and openness to the other. It was grace for me. Yet that family had certainly experienced the discipline demanded by displacement, illness, grief. I have often said that I don't know how to give in a vacuum. Virtue isn't something we develop in order to do something else. Virtue is called forth when we respond to the need of another. The discipline is encounter, and virtues develop from that.

For Herb, persistence is a virtue of an ecumenical heart.

Since I retired a bit more than two years ago I've had time to pursue some hobbies that took second place during my years as a pastor, teacher and bishop. My most avid hobby is gardening, both flower and vegetable. I've transformed a very ordinary looking yard to one that is so beautiful that I was invited to include it in a garden tour in mid-July. Part of every day is spent among the blooms and veggies.

As any good gardener knows, one of the keys to successful gardening is a compost pile. Behind my hobby greenhouse, tucked discreetly among the trees, but open to the sun, is a series of four compost bins, each in a different stage of "development." Compost piles are an ugly sight to those who don't appreciate what's going on in those bins. Grass clippings, potato and carrot peelings, banana skins, orange rinds, dead fish from the lake shore, rotten fruit, soiled Kleenex, rotting leaves, and much more. In a carefully concealed corner I keep a rusty coffee can where I collect urine, saving the septic system and giving my compost a steady supply of uric acid to speed the process of decomposition.

No, a compost heap is not a pleasant thing to behold. But when properly managed, it produces no smell and periodically gives one a marvelous supply of rich, dark soil to add to the vegetable and flower gardens, keeping the earth soft and friable—the conditions for a steady supply of succulent produce and spectacular blooms.

Walt Whitman must have been a gardener. He wrote words that I have scrawled on a rough sign and posted in the midst of my compost piles. It reminds our visitors that what they see should be judged with respect:

> Behold this compost!
>
> Behold it well!
>
> It grows such sweet things
>
> From such corruptions . . .

My compost piles are to me a parable of the ecumenical virtue of persistence and illustrate why it is one of the crucial virtues of an ecumenical heart.

My more-than-quarter-century involvement in ecumenical affairs has many parallels to my compost pile. Much of the time it hasn't looked very pleasant. In fact, it is the hardest—at times the least-rewarding—work I've done during my active ministry. Sparse attendance at meetings, lack of interest, resistance to change, ennui, misunderstanding, self-interest, ambition, lack of money, denominational differences and indifference—these and much more have made the ecumenical enterprise look rather hopeless at times. "How can any good come from this?" I have asked again and again.

But as with so many of life's ventures, time and persistence at the task give one a different perspective. I have learned that there are good outcomes for those who persist, who endure setbacks and disappointments.

There is a breakthrough now and then. Believers once separated and suspicious, when brought together in the same arena, discover that their differences, when blended and properly managed, produce a sweet and productive outcome.

Persistence, like the composting process, pays off in the long run. It does so for at least two reasons. The first is quite mysterious. Like the breaking down of contrasting elements in nature, persistent dialogue and conversation between believers is the means by which the Spirit of God works for unity and love among them. As Reuel Howe put it years ago, there is "miracle in dialogue." We don't need to analyze it or insist on understanding exactly how it happens, any more than I understand the action going on secretly, day and night, season after season, in my compost pile. Simply let it happen. "The wind blows where it will . . ."

But there is a second element. Just as a compost pile must be constantly fed and turned, so we go about the ecumenical task with deliberation and attention to detail. We assign to our leaders, our ecumenical officers and their staffs, the task of "working at" the process. We may not always like what they add and sometimes we may think they worked too hard at turning things over. But unless they are deliberate and careful, they run the risk of venturing out in directions the churches won't follow.

Persistence as a virtue is more than patience. Patience can be aimless, allowing things to happen without attention to what is going on. William Barclay, in writing about patience as a fruit of the Spirit, says it must be thought of as "patience with a purpose." For believers who take the Scripture as their source and guide for living, the purpose must be what Christ envisioned: "That they may be one."

Exactly what it means to "be one" is something we cannot know in advance. Our commission is to be engaged in the process. The outcome will surprise us at times, more often than not evolving in directions we could not have imagined. At times it may issue in formal statements of agreement, in organizational merger, in official recognition of ministries, in interim sacramental celebrations, or, as with the decision of the Reformed churches and the Evangelical Lutheran Church in America in 1997, "full communion." More often than not, however, it will be hard to quantify.

Improved relations in a community, friendships across denominational lines, cooperation in service projects, interfaith educational programs, and much more—none of these things, formal or informal, will happen unless we tend to the process, adding to and stimulating the interaction of all elements of the ecumenical endeavor.

I am reminded of the tireless and often thankless efforts of some of the pioneers. Since I knew one of them, let me use him as an illustration. Dr. Bernhard Christiansen was president of Augsburg College in Minneapolis when I was a student on that campus in the early 1950s. He was one of the first Lutheran leaders and theologians to engage in informal conversations between Lutherans and Roman Catholics. When these visits became known in his small, conservative Lutheran church body, he was severely criticized for "talking to those Catholics."

But Christiansen bore the criticism patiently and quietly continued his involvement with the Benedictine community at Saint John's Abbey. His courage inspired other visionaries to join him. Messy and often disjointed as it was, the process gradually changed a few minds here and there. Though it took decades, and though they could not have known its outcome, their persistence produced the fruit we enjoy today.

Even more important, their example serves to remind us that we never "arrive" in this venture. When the flowers bloom with profusion and the vegetables bear in abundance, the gardener knows that they will only continue to prosper if more good nutrients from the compost pile are added year after year. There is always more to do. If future generations are to benefit from the ongoing process of ecumenism, we must be as persistent as the pioneers.

A familiar Gospel text is the parable of the soils—another earthy analogy. What waste! What useless effort! What discouragement to watch the precious seed eaten, scorched, and choked out. Yet, the seeding went on because the sower believed his persistent efforts would bring results.

We can also learn from the biblical "heroes of the faith" whom the author of the Letter to the Hebrews writes about. Every one of them had a reason to be depressed and discouraged. They wondered about the outcome. The litany of their trials makes one ask how any of them survived. But they did, by God's grace. And the outcome of their persistence was something they themselves never saw—"All these, though they were commended for their faith, did not receive what was promised." But those who followed reaped the benefits—"since God had provided something better so that they would not, apart from us, be made perfect" (Hebrews 11:39-40).

We are here these days because folks like Bernhard Christiansen and Kilian McDonnell and Warren Quanbeck and Bob Bilheimer and a host of other ecumenical visionaries did not give up when the venture seemed to be going nowhere. And unless we continue the venture, others will be deprived in years to come of the benefits that may come to them.

What Thomas Merton said in his book *Contemplative Prayer* could also be said about the virtues for an ecumenical heart. If we bear with hardship in prayer and wait patiently for the time of grace, we may well discover that meditation and prayer are very joyful experiences. We should not, however, judge the value of our meditation by "how we feel." A hard and apparently fruitless meditation may in fact be much more valuable than one that is easy, happy, enlightened, and apparently a big success.

The same can be said about ecumenism. It can indeed look very messy and disorganized at times, seeming to promise no positive results. Yet "a hard and apparently fruitless" process may produce results that will surprise and delight us.

A prayer from the Lutheran Book of Worship seems appropriate when reflecting on persistence as a virtue of the ecumenical heart:

> O Lord, you have called your servants to ventures of which we cannot see the ending, by paths as yet untrodden, through perils unknown. Give us faith to go out with good courage, not knowing where we go, but only that your hand is leading us and your love supporting us. Through Jesus Christ our Lord. Amen.

Further thinking:

1. What are you going to do with the rest of your life?

2. Share a story about meals in your family.

3. What has been hard work that has been worth working for?

4. Discuss how you learned about hospitality.

Chapter 9

Envisioning Hope

"For just as the body is one and has many members,
and all the members of the body, though many, are one body,
so it is with Christ. For in one Spirit we are all baptized into
one body—Jews or Gentiles, slaves or free—and we were all
made to drink of one Spirit."
1 Corinthians 12:12-13

Neighborhood requires that we trust our neighbors, and trust requires that we believe they are people—like us, bursting with hopes and secrets and fears, longing to be happy. Trust may mean withholding judgment, or working again and again to clear up misunderstandings. The neighbor, if not already a friend, is a friend to be.

In addition to trust, though, imagination helps, and humor does too. Gary displays imagination and humor, as well as love for Chicago, in his metaphor for Church.

> The metaphor of the Body of Christ has dominated ecumenical thinking. For many theologians, it is *the* model of Church. They appeal to a strong authority: Paul in his letters to Corinth and Rome.

But what if "body" were interpreted more as "body politic" than as an individual human body? What if we look at the Church as a heavenly Chicago?

What? "The city that works" (with a boss mayor and lots of patronage jobs)? The city with broad shoulders, hog butcher to the world, with the attendant dirt, crime, racism, and poverty—not to mention some awful sports teams (the Bulls being the divine exception)? What is so heavenly about Chicago?

Well, the Chicago area was home to me for most of my life. I've been gone for five years, and although I enjoy my new home, I still think Chicago has much to commend itself as a metaphor for the Church.

Chicago is a city of neighborhoods. If we were to clean up the racism, classism, ethnocentrism, and the like, what would we have? We have a city of neighborhoods, each with a distinct identity: food, music, language, art, customs, governance. Residents are proud of their roots and want others to see the best of their culture.

Each neighborhood is a community with rich relationships and with wealth enough to go around. People live in the neighborhood because they like the culture and the community, not because they are trapped by race or by class. Visitors know they have come to a different place and are warmly welcomed by the residents.

The neighborhoods relate together in a council that deliberates on matters affecting the common good. Conflict can occur at any level; human beings are not angels, knowing intuitively what is right and flawlessly acting on their perfect knowledge. We converse, deliberate, see partially, disagree, fight. And we can—in the midst of our conflicts, while vigorously disagreeing about intractable or fundamental issues, without demanding that each person become like me or agree with me—hospitably offer each other our foods, our wisdoms, our works of beauty.

For me, such would be a heavenly place to live, a worthy metaphor of the way the Church could be.

Tim thinks good cooks and a little imagination will carry ecumenism a long way.

If ecumenism were a food, how would it taste?

Some imagine it as the religious equivalent of pabulum. You know what I mean, "baby food." The "Complete Turkey Dinner for Infants" conjures up mouth-watering images of roast turkey, steaming rolls, brown gravy, succulent pies, and cool cranberry sauce. What one gets in the jar is the result of pureeing those dishes into a medium-thick, brownish gruel with a faint red tinge. Every bite is the same—guaranteed the same—consistency, the same temperature, the same taste. No lumps or bumps. No unexpected surprises for Junior—it might upset his fragile digestive system. In fact, without the label, few adults could identify any of the gruel's original ingredients. Poor Junior. What would he say about baby food if he could only talk?

I can image a different sort of ecumenism, one acceptable to even the religious gourmands among us. This kind of meal requires fresh ingredients: bread from the baker, today's catch from the wharf, and vegetables from grandma's garden out back. It needs spices that have been carefully stored, separate and in sealed containers. The pepper and parmesan are always freshly ground. The elements of the meal are creatively combined just before serving, still hot off the grill. The milk is cold enough to cause condensation on the glasses, the coffee always recently roasted, just ground, served fresh and piping hot. Now, doesn't that sound more appetizing than Junior's baby food?

Here are some basic rules for good ecumenical cooking:

- First, individual ingredients must be fresh, not canned and not spoiled.

- Second, don't reject ingredients simply because they come from unusual places. Truffles are rooted out of the ground by pigs in France. Caviar comes from the stomachs of Russian sturgeon. Head cheese is, well, let's move on.

- Third, would-be chefs must learn about and appreciate the unique characteristics of each ingredient in order to use it artfully.

- Fourth, unexpected combinations often result in great dishes: chocolate and peanut butter, chicken and cashews, raisins and rice. Don't be afraid to experiment!

Every religious tradition preserves many things of value. Like various foods and spices, some of these are best stored separately. Elements from them can and should be combined judiciously and creatively, just before serving. Borrowing from another tradition need not mean religious pureeing. Vary the dishes. Serve different meals. Change the menu with the diners and the seasons. Each congregation will have different tastes and certainly its own favorite dishes.

Remember, some wonderful combinations may be completely unexpected. A Latin beat could add an unexpected zing to a familiar European hymn. Combining Italian pasta with New World tomatoes might result in a mouth-watering liturgy. How about a succulent sermon, served *al dente,* graced with chopped almonds from the rainforest? Can you imagine a prayer so good it reminds a congregation of the aroma of bittersweet chocolate from the Americas, served with coffee from the West Indies? Ahhh!

See, ecumenism can be tasty! We just need good cooks and a little imagination.

Who would think that jazz has something to say about ecumenism? But watch as Brian develops his metaphor.

Is it true that jazz musicians can pick notes out of thin air? Jazz artists commonly perform without scores, without a conductor to coordinate their performances, and can play the same piece differently every time. In some cases, they have never met before, yet they seem to share a common spirit.

Contributing further to the jazz mystique is the transient and unique nature of jazz creations. Each performance's evolving ideas, sustained momentarily by air waves, vanish as new developments overtake them, seemingly never to be repeated. That jazz performers improvise their music, a common explanation for these marvels, begs the more difficult question: Just what is the nature of this improvisation?

Jazz performers often make the music look so easy. In fact, the formation of jazz musicians is just as much a part of the story as the performance. Training and rigorous musical thinking underlie improvisation. The creative processes that lie at the heart of the culture of jazz are grounded in a history and tradition of development. Intimate accounts of artistic growth from childhood to old age portray the deeply creative experiences that engage artists, revealing a serious, ongoing preoccupation with the music and the music-making that define their lives.

What, if anything, can this contribute to the conversation about ecumenism? Ecumenical work calls on the participants to improvise. This improvisation utilizes the kind of processes that jazz performers know well. A melody and a harmonic progression shape the direction. Each performer is encouraged to play with this melody, utilizing particular gifts and skills. And each musician is essential to the group. In the midst of the playing, other performers seek to enhance what each player is offering

The creative exchange builds on itself, and further performers intentionally borrow and rework what has preceded. The music is a dance. The form enhances the functional melody. The complexity of the melody and harmonic progression determines, to some extent, the amount of familiarity that is needed to make the music sing. You've got to listen attentively to the exchange and interchange between performers.

Ecumenism is a similar dance. At times, the melody and mission are clear and simple. Cooperative and shared ministries beg to be sounded and initiated. Sometimes the composition is a bit more challenging. The melody is complex and the progression is complicated, requiring more rehearsal and more listening. The dialogues between national Church bodies sometimes engage the conversation in this way.

And it's not just that small groups are easy and large ones hard. Relationships between spouses in an ecumenical marriage, or the heartfelt positions held passionately by neighboring churches, require much listening and exchange. At times, the conversations between denominations are quite simple and straight-forward. The task, of course, is to discern the complexity of the situation and the calling of God. It takes a lot of practice to improvise.

So if, as philosophers suggest, the limits of language are the limits of our world, bringing the language and metaphor of jazz alongside ecumenism expands those limits and suggests a fresh perspective, a unity based on exchanging gifts and mutual mission on common ground. Ecumenists often pick their notes out of thin air. In most cases, they also have been listening to the music that has been calling toward unity. Keeping jazz in mind is helpful, because it expands the focus not only to include product and goal, formal documents and agreements, but also to begin to recognize the *process* of ecumenism.

From Chicago to food to jazz: each metaphor gives us a different way of seeing ecumenism. All of them have hope hidden behind the humor. Sometimes hope is more naked, as it is for Robert.

It was a good day for church. The day was something of a special occasion, the feast of Saints Peter and Paul. I was at church with a group of friends from various religious traditions: Presbyterian, Episcopalian, Orthodox, Roman Catholic, and Church of the Nazarene. In several days of conversation we had discovered in each other and in ourselves a number of virtues that drew our hearts together before God, in spite of and often because of our own traditions. Attendance at Mass seemed an appropriate way to celebrate our togetherness.

The service was jubilant. The praises we sang with gusto. The thanksgivings we prayed with fervor. The

Scripture readings told of two apostles, Peter and Paul, who, though their ministries had different characteristics, together served Christ's Church. How like us!

We were supremely joyful until I realized that not all of us would be able to celebrate the Eucharist together. The happiness that I had expected was now mixed with discouragement. We were about to be reminded that the solidarity that we had experienced was only partial.

My Orthodox friend and I slipped out to the side during the Communion procession. A few moments later one of the Roman Catholics of our company was returning from having received Eucharist, and the three of us, Roman Catholic, Orthodox, and Protestant, looked at each other with tears of sorrow and found ourselves suspended in time. We recognized in each other the profound disparity between what we believed and how we could practice it. We had been sharing our hearts all week and had in a significant way united ourselves to each other, but at that moment we felt the impact of the disunity of Christ's Church. We were distanced by the very celebration that was instituted to bring us together.

Ten months later I joined the full communion of the Roman Catholic Church, and a month later I visited my family in Colorado. I had missed my brother's high school graduation, but I wasn't about to miss this, his graduation from college. And what delight to visit my family during Mother's Day weekend! Sunday arrived, and we all—mom, brother, and sister-in-law—went to Mass in a rural parish church. The bliss of the community was invigorating, and their hospitality was warm. The simplicity of the music and prayers communicated the gospel vividly.

But I will not soon forget the sadness in my brother's face when I explained to him why they would not be able to come to the Table. "It implies a unity in the Church that does not exist," I said. It is what I had been told earlier.

I would have given anything at that moment for unity. I now found myself on the other side of the fence, able to celebrate Eucharist while others could not. The pain that I experienced as I journeyed to the altar alone is inexpressible. I had felt this isolation before, but now I was being distanced from my family. My mother and brother could not feast with me in the most important meal the Church offers.

"Some day," I keep hoping. Some day we will no longer be separated. We will join together at the Table. We will no longer see through a glass darkly. We will realize what it means to be the Body of Christ.

Our backgrounds, our training, our experiences, the people we know, all play into how we see our religious tradition. More than that, they also affect the hope we have for our Church—or our lack of hope. Humor, imagination, sensitivity, all can help us to build our hope and the hope of others.

Looking back and looking forward, put your own imagination to work.

Further thinking:

1. Imagine a metaphor for Church that expresses your experience or your dreams.

2. In places you have lived, where has there been a spirit of ecumenism and what has brought it into being?

3. How does ecumenism taste to you?

4. What do you hope for your church and its relations with other churches in your community? How can you be a part of it?

Afterword

"You are the God who works wonders . . ."
Psalm 77:14

These stories from ordinary Christians were experienced, shared, and recorded prior to the fall of 2001 when the impact of isolation and ignorance, arrogance and hatred, lack of understanding and dialogue became more fully realized by many. The spirit of ecumenism celebrated and explored in this book and in many communities is a hopeful gift Christians can offer a broken-hearted world.

Rooted deeply within the Christian story, ecumenism resists definition, but as one participant put it, "You know it when you see it."

You know it when you see it in the words and stories and life of Jesus. He continuously calls us to erase boundaries, love enemies, welcome strangers.

You know it when you see it as diverse Christians from your hometown gather to sing hymns, bury a friend, or share a meal.

You know it when you see it when you see the curiosity and energy of teenagers lead them to explore the stories and traditions of others through a Habitat for Humanity project.

You know it when you see it when people meet across denominational lines for Bible study.

You know it when you see it as different churches gather to pray for peace.

While Christians lay claim to ecumenism as a Christian movement, nurturing an ecumenical heart is a way of living and being in the world for *all* of us. It may be the *only* way to live as neighbors—as God's people—on the planet we share. Mary Jane was quick to point out, "I don't think you have to be a Christian to have this heart." When Christians gather with Muslims and Jews and others to share stories and build trust, ecumenical hearts are at work.

"What virtues ready a person for an ecumenical heart?" Dan's question is an important one to revisit—again and again. There are virtue books in the bookstores these days, but they may not include the virtues embedded in our stories or those of others with an ecumenical spirit. There is a tension about which virtues are most virtuous.

Gary says that autonomy and self-sufficiency, highly-valued virtues in American culture, are *not* ecumenical virtues; recognizing our need for one another *is*. Ecumenical hearts are courageous and imaginative, encourage openness rather than self-preservation, approach others with humility not pride. Ecumenical hearts forgive, receive, question, change, and trust. Practicing virtues needed for twenty-first-century relationships and situations is risk-taking, but Christianity is not about safety. Jesus teaches us to walk across the street, step onto the water, speak in tongues, reach across divisions, love our enemies.

Susan shared that "virtues are called forth as we respond to the need of another." How we respond effects the shaping of the heart, "Developing an ecumenical heart is like the water that begins a waterfall—a drop at a time," Brian wrote. Ecumenism is hard work and an awesome responsibility, sometimes calling us to enter relationships and dialogues in which we never imagined ourselves.

In a broken world we are called to practice:

the *gratitude* of Stefanie's friend with cancer,
Robert's *"pursuit of a holy or authentic life,"*
Dan's *honesty* and *self-awareness,*
Elena's *compassion,*
the *nonjudgmentalism* that reached across 1600 years,
  language and gender to Roberta,
the *humor* of Vera's family which reminds them not to
  take themselves too seriously,
trusting, as Tim does, in the Spirit,
Curt's *skepticism* and *curiosity*—("If you have questions . . . you are our kind of guy."),
Herb's compost pile *patience* and *persistence,*
Susan's *"walking in another's footsteps . . . seeing what
  they see."*
Alva's *slowing down,* allowing this to become clearer.

In a disconnected world, there is hope in:

Maggie's ancient tradition *welcoming* a curious, young
  boy,
Granny Lindsey's power of *love,*
Patrick's friend, Bob Piper, wisely *overlooking things,*
Gary's sense of *incompletion,*
Mary Jane's faith in our ability to *"see with an artist's
  eye,"*
Carol's *celebrating* parts of the journey,

Anwar Sadat's refusal to "accept reality as it had been handed to him. He *imagined* what couldn't be, and once he had done so, everything changed."

In a suspicious world, Brian's grandmother teaches us what it means to be Christ-like and welcome the stranger.

My grandmother demonstrated by example what it means to share an ecumenical heart. I remember that my grandfather was extremely disappointed with a neighbor who had cut down a hedge too short. They probably even "had words" about it. I'm sure that they were avoiding each other. Yet my grandmother was always open to the serendipity of the moment. She was always preparing. On Sundays, after she had set the lunch table, for instance, she would keep extra place settings ready in the kitchen in case someone stopped by unexpectedly during lunch. She would whisk those settings to the table before visitors even got to the kitchen, and then, to their surprise, it appeared that they were anticipated.

So I remember the Sunday when the hedge-trimming neighbor appeared at the door during lunch. My grandfather went grumbling to the door but was reminded by my grandmother to be sure to invite the neighbor to lunch. Grandma ran to the kitchen and immediately had the table set for "one more." I can still see the surprise on the neighbor's face when he walked to the table and it appeared that we were waiting just for him.

A place at the table, friend or foe, neighbor or stranger—this is what my Grandma taught me—all are welcome.

What virtues ready a person for an ecumenical heart? Who has nurtured these virtues in you throughout your life? How do you nurture them in others? Pose these questions to groups within your church—children and adults, diverse groups of Christians, or an interfaith group. This book can be a starting point for telling your own stories and creating ways in which your community might foster an ecumenical spirit.

Stefanie says that "ecumenism must always take place on the person-to-person level where the intimacy of Jesus' touch and healing may take place though us as flesh-and-blood persons who hear and see and accept and care for each other." Have extra food and place settings on hand for unexpected guests. It shouldn't take a tornado or falling buildings for us to recognize our common story, our connectedness and need for one another—and even our beautiful and complicated differences.

One woman who was not a participant, but who read the stories, shared that the "ecumenical heart needs a sense of watching for what new thing God is about to do." A heart for ecumenism is mindful, watchful, and open to surprise. Tim, in searching for God, was surprised to find God's people. Share a cup of coffee with your neighbor and enjoy the surprises. As Tilden Edwards wrote at the beginning of this book, "We can trust that God's Spirit will be alive in such sharing . . ."

Storytellers

Alva Baker is the owner of Baker Consulting Associates. Her expertise includes strategic business planning, economic analysis, market research, marketing, public relations, and community outreach. Alva earned her A.B. from Boston University and her M.B.A. at the University of Southern California.

Robert Brindle is a doctoral candidate in biblical studies at The Catholic University of America in Washington, D.C. In addition to completing his doctoral studies, Robert is currently working as the finance manager for Nazarene Compassionate Ministries in Kansas City, Missouri.

Roberta Bondi teaches the history of the early Church, spirituality, and Julian of Norwich at Candler School of theology, Emory University in Atlanta, Georgia.

Magdaline (Maggie) Bovis is an American Orthodox and an ecumenist. Maggie graduated as a science major and spent most of her professional life as a researcher in neurochemistry at the University of Minnesota.

Herbert W. Chilstrom is the former presiding bishop of the Evangelical Lutheran Church in America. He was its first leader after the formation of the ELCA in 1987 and served until 1995. He has advanced degrees from the

Lutheran School of Theology at Chicago, Princeton Theological Seminary, and New York University.

Mary Jane Taylor Crook graduated from the University of Texas at Austin. She is currently executive assistant in the Communications Department of The Metropolitan Museum of Art in New York City.

Elena Delgado is a graduate of Mary Baldwin College in Staunton, Virginia, and continued graduate studies in the Presbyterian School of Christian Education in Richmond, Virginia. She was ordained to the ministry of Word and Sacrament in 1999 and presently serves the Orchard Park (N.Y.) Presbyterian Church as interim pastor.

Vera Duncanson lives in Champaign, Illinois, with her husband, Tom, a teacher. Since 1986 Vera has worked at Provena Covenant Medical Center as Roman Catholic Pastoral Minister, primarily in the areas of oncology, hospice, and bereavement.

Patrick Henry has been executive director of the Institute for Ecumenical and Cultural Research since 1984. Previously, he taught for seventeen years in the Religion Department at Swarthmore College in Pennsylvania.

Timothy P. Jenney is an ordained Assemblies of God (Pentecostal) minister. He has served several congregations as senior pastor, been a professor of New Testament at the college level, and traveled and taught abroad.

Brian Johnson serves as a chaplain at Gustavus Adolphus College in St. Peter, Minnesota, and as artistic director for Christmas in Christ Chapel. A 1980 graduate of Gustavus, Brian completed his M.Div. at Luther Northwestern Seminary in St. Paul. He lectures at Luther Seminary in the area of liturgy, and is a writer for *Sundays and Seasons* published by Augsburg Fortress.

G. Daniel Little became interested in urban ministry while a student at McCormick Seminary from which he graduated in 1954. From 1996 through 1999 Dan helped two large Presbyterian churches in pastoral transitions: Village Church, Prairie Village, Kansas, and Westminster Church, Minneapolis. He and his wife Joan retired in Madison, Wisconsin.

Gary E. Peluso-Verdend is director of Church relations and associate professor of practical theology at Garrett-Evangelical Theological Seminary in Evanston, Illinois. He is an elder in the Northern Illinois Conference of the United Methodist Church. He earned his B.A. in religion from Carroll College, his M.Div. from Garrett-Evangelical Theological Seminary, and his Ph.D. in practical theology from the University of Chicago.

Nancy Hastings Sehested is a Baptist preacher and storyteller. She received her M.Div. from Union Theological Seminary in New York City in 1978. She was ordained in a Southern Baptist Church in Memphis in 1981. She is also a co-pastor for a new ecumenical church in Asheville called Circle of Mercy.

Carol McGee Stiles is a "cradle" Presbyterian and an elder, and a member of the First Presbyterian Church of Foley, Minnesota. Carol currently serves on the board of directors of The Institute for Ecumenical and Cultural Research as its chair.

Stefanie Weisgram, O.S.B., is a member of Saint Benedict's Monastery, St. Joseph, Minnesota. Her degrees are from the College of Saint Benedict, Middlebury College, Dominican University, and St. John's University. Her present ministry is primarily as the Collection Development Librarian for the College of Saint Benedict and St. John's University in Minnesota. She was also the reviews editor for *Sisters Today*.

Susan K. Wood, s.c.l., a member of the Sisters of Charity of Leavenworth, Kansas, is currently professor of theology and associate dean in the School of Theology, St. John's University, Collegeville, Minnesota. She publishes frequently on ecumenical topics.

Curt Yaws is a commercial real estate investor and property manager, operating a portfolio of business properties in the Kansas City and San Diego areas. He graduated from Baylor University, receiving bachelor's and master's degrees in business.